Born in Glasgow, Jean Barbour Clark was the eldest of three children. Her family moved to the suburbs just before World War II when she was four years old. Her grandfather and aunt joined the family for their own safety and also to support her mother when her father joined the armed forces.

Jean became a Christian in her early teens through an organisation that valued ministry to children. Over the years, she was inspired by their ingenuity and creativity to develop her own children's work.

To my late husband, Bobby. Only he could have put up with the upheaval of being married to me.

I wish to thank all the friends and relatives who spurred me on when times were difficult and cheered me on when things went well.

Table of Contents

Foreword

Since I arrived at Easterhouse Baptist Church in 1990, Jean Clark has been a person who really impressed. Her love and dedication for children and children's work has been clear to see. And she combines that with a no-nonsense straightforward approach to life and dealing with people which I very much admire... although some people can find it challenging at times!

But this book has opened my eyes to a lot more of Jean's life and experiences. I see it as being in the same style as Mollie Weir's series including Shoes were for Sunday which opened my eyes to the Glasgow of my parents and earlier times. Jean follows that style of writing with a book that is highly readable, funny, poignant, moving and with some serious lessons for us all along the way. Of course, Jean Clark's book has a spiritual dimension which points us to the God who loves young children more than any of us could ever do.

Right from the introduction Jean makes it clear that God had and has a plan for her life... and for each one of us. She speaks of her shock at some of the poverty she encountered in Glasgow as a youngster – something I could identify with having seen children and families living right on the breadline in Nepal. There were no fussy eaters at that time; "those kids were happy to eat anything. Every plate was cleared."

There is something about Jean Clark more than just her own personal dedication and self-sacrifice. Throughout her life she has clearly had a huge impact on other people, encouraging them too to support work with young people by making donations or in other ways. "The waitresses we had seen... turned up with bags of clothes. They had noticed some of the children... didn't have a jacket or a coat. These lovely ladies kitted them out." And clearly it was Jean Clark and her dedication which had impacted on those around her.

Jean's dedication and enthusiasm could be formidable at times – "There was no stopping me!" And clearly some people did not react well at times, "Suddenly, an angry voiced boomed... 'Whit right huv you tae tell ma weans...?'." And yet the same person would later say to Jean, "Ah want tae apologise... You did aw that work..."

Jean is also very open about her own feelings and her relationship with Jesus Christ. She can speak of how at one point she was in a 'flood of despair and embarrassment'. But then again how God and His word in the Bible would speak to her and encourage her, "The good man does not escape all troubles – he has them too. But the Lord helps him in each and every one."

This is not a long book. There are excellent illustrations by Jean's daughter Beverly which draw you in. It is easily ready, at times funny, at times deeply personal. But if you are interested in Glasgow, in God's love for young people, and in how he can use an ordinary person to do great things, then I would very highly recommend it.

– John Mason, MSP for Glasgow Shettleston

Preface

Kintsugi is a centuries old Japanese method of repairing broken pottery by filling in the cracks with gold. The result is a pot which you can see has obviously been mended and would otherwise be worthless, but is now a thing of beauty and value.

Every child in our care, in whatever circumstances, comes to us with a certain number of little cracks in their emotions, whether caused by being misunderstood, chastened too severely, or let down in some way by an adult or some other child.

These cracks can widen as they get older, but every children's worker has the job of filling in the cracks, using the Kintsugi method — filling the life of each child with golden moments and times to treasure that make the fragile vessel more beautiful and much stronger. If you are a children's worker, a youth worker or even a parent, it is hoped that this memoire will encourage you. And may the reading of it remind you of golden moments in the jigsaw of your own life which you can pass on to the children in your care.

Introduction

You would have called Miss Dalby a very plain woman. She was quite tall and slender with slightly prominent front teeth and a way of pulling in her head and looking from side to side that made her appear to have a double chin. Her greying hair was pulled back tightly in a bun and she was easily embarrassed, old-fashioned and modest. But she was always positive and was not afraid to laugh at herself which endeared her to each one of us.

The Missionary Training School was being disbanded as was the youth club they organised. Everyone who worked there would soon be unemployed — Miss Dalby included. She was growing more and more concerned not only about her own situation but also about the future of the young people she had been mentoring. What would the future hold? Would we find another Christian fellowship to be part of? Or would we just find this an opportunity to forget about God and all things religious?

She decided to call all the teenagers to prayer. As we entered the little assembly room she was already kneeling in prayer at her chair, so we quietly did likewise.

I cannot say exactly what she prayed but it went something like this: "Lord, I know you have a special path for these young people to follow. You have a special work for them to do." And at that point something in me gave a leap. It was unmistakeable. "God had a plan for me." I didn't know where He was going to lead me or even when it would be, but I was assured at that moment that as long as I stayed near to Him then He would guide me every step of the way.

In later years, when I felt downhearted and full of doubts, that moment when my heart missed a beat would remind me that I was not on my own.

Our Heavenly Father also had a plan for dear Miss Dalby, because shortly after our meeting she went to be in charge of a hostel for young nurses in training. It was a live-in post and she spent her remaining working years there. No one could have been more appropriate. She had been a nurse herself when she was younger and would be able to empathise with all the young girls in her care.

Chapter 1
The Gorbals

I was quite unprepared for my first glimpse of Glasgow's Gorbals that winter of 1950. I had lived most of my 15 years in a suburban terraced house which nestled on the lush green banks of the River Cart.

I was already familiar with tenement life as I often visited relatives in the big city. Many of them had all their worldly goods contained in just two compact rooms. I marvelled at their tidiness and admired their spotless linoleum floors, their gleaming cooking ranges and bleached white 'wally' sinks. Nobody, but nobody would dare to put a mark on their common close walls or leave so much as a sweet paper on their pipe-clayed stairs.

Aunty Bella, my grandfather's sister, was so house-proud I was almost afraid to sit on her highly polished chairs. Not a single speck of dust was allowed to settle. And she seemed to have a rolled-up newspaper permanently in her hand to swot any insect that inadvertently swooped through her open windows; to do such a thing was instant death!

But I was to find out that tenement life in Nicholson Street could be very different. I followed my two missionary friends into one of the closes. The proximity of the building in the next street diminished the daylight from the stair-head window to such an extent, that we had to stop for a few seconds to enable our eyes to adjust to the darkness. The air smelt foul. Dampness seemed to permeate every nook and cranny and I held my breath as the musty odour filled my nostrils.

The stairs were chipped and worn, so we walked very gingerly, holding on to the rusty wrought iron banisters for support. A youth scurried from a door on the first landing and I gasped as the smell of urine and human excrement escaped from the common lavatory.

My companions opened another door and led me into a large hallway.

"Should you not have knocked?" I asked uncertainly.

They laughed and one explained, "Each door here leads to the home of a different family." So it seems that what was once a flat belonging to a well-to-do family was now the dwelling place of five families. I was stunned.

A door opened and, evidently expecting us, a pale thin woman ushered us in. As we entered the room, we were immediately assailed by a smell.

I was soon to become very familiar with. Damp, dog, stale tobacco smoke, sweat — all united in a stench that made me want to turn on my heels. But then I saw the children…it was love at first sight.

Two small boys were playing with marbles in a corner, completely absorbed in their contest, their clothes were grubby and worn and their short trousers revealed little thin legs that had not seen soap and water for some time, but they seemed happy wee boys for all that.

A lovely little girl hung on to her mother's apron as she eyed us shyly. Her hair held me in its spell. It would have been the most beautiful golden colour if only it had been washed. It evidently hadn't been combed for days and so the curls were matted and tangled. Her little eyes seemed to search out mine as we steadily gazed at one another.

A toddler slid off his father's knee and smiling he staggered uncertainly towards us. All he wore was a little vest. His bare feet were extremely dirty and his bottom and legs were blotched with cold, but no one seemed to notice or care. I wanted to wrap him up in a warm blanket and take him home.

I discovered later that it was quite common for little tots to go about half dressed. It saved having to constantly wash nappies. Visits to the Steamie were expensive when you were living on Public Assistance, and many of the back court washhouses were in such disrepair that people were unable to use them. The effort of boiling kettles for water, scrubbing clothes by hand and hanging garments to dry everywhere, eventually became such drudgery, that many of the mothers already weakened by a poor diet, gradually gave up the struggle to keep everything and everyone clean.

The missionaries chatted warmly to the woman. They had evidently visited this family before. They introduced me as one of their helpers and handing over a package one whispered, "We thought the children could use some of these things." The mother accepted the parcel awkwardly, glancing quickly at her husband, and as he glared at us over his newspaper the other missionary added tactfully, "If you can't make use of them yourself, perhaps you'll know someone else who can." Gratefully, the mother assured us she would find a use for whatever they had brought and then in the wake of her thanks and cheerios' we descended the grimy litter-strewn stairway and made our way to the Mission's new premises at 190 Nicholson Street.

The Mission had acquired a Main Door flat in the Gorbals in the hope that their presence on the doorstep of such poverty would make a difference. It had three bedrooms, a kitchen/living room and a large room (probably the parlour in its heyday) which was to be used for their public meetings. I could see at a glance that this had once been the home of a very posh family who had lived there in Edwardian grandeur. It even had a bathroom complete with Bath, W.C., and Wash Basin, each adorned with a beautiful floral decoration and still in good working order.

The flat had been sold to the Mission by owners Mr and Mrs Wallace on the understanding that they would continue living on the premises as cleaner/caretakers in lieu of rent.

They were an unusual couple. Mr Wallace was tall, quiet and deeply religious. He was a freelance painter and decorator and when at home he had the odd habit of walking from room to room, reading his Bible, and when he read something that excited his imagination he would cry out 'Hallelujah' or 'Praise the Lord' and laugh to himself. He was seldom at home because when he wasn't plying his trade, he was visiting Missions and Churches as a lay preacher. Mrs Wallace, on the other hand, was always at home. She was friendly and open-hearted and I took to her immediately. She was to become a dear friend and confidante.

Because of my blossoming friendship with Mrs Wallace my visits to the Gorbals were eventually not restricted to Sundays or the mid-week service. On many a night we would sit by the fire and chat about anything and everything.

My mother worried about me spending so much time in such a notorious area. "Are you not afraid something will happen to you?" she would say worriedly, knowing how afraid I was of so many other things, like death and the dark, spiders and wasps, frogs and horses. I still found it difficult to go upstairs alone at night to my bedroom and here I was visiting a place where it was alleged thieves lurked and murderers hid.

But strangely I felt safer walking down the Gorbals streets than in those of my more salubrious housing estate where the streets were deserted in the evenings and thick hedges surrounded the gardens, adding to the terrifying sense of isolation when walking there at night.

The Gorbals streets, on the other hand, were teeming with life. There was a Public House on almost every corner — not your soft lights and sweet music type of Pub, but the spit and sawdust kind, with a strictly male clientele. When their money ran out the men would stand on the pavement outside the Pub. Some leaned against the wall reading their newspapers, others engaged in small talk. They called out to friends and family passing by and those with a few coppers to spare would surreptitiously place a bet with the local bookie's runner (against the law in those days). There could be as many as 10 or 20 men standing on the corner outside each Pub, even in the cold and rain. Having seen the conditions they were living in, I came to understand why they would think this preferable to spending every night with their families in the suffocating confines of a single room.

Children played outdoors until well after dark. They scurried about laughing, jumping, skipping, arguing or darting in and out of closes playing Hide and Seek. They threw phrases into the air that echoed down the street.

"The game's a bogey!"

"You're hett!"

"It's your turn tae caw!"

"Ah'm no' playin' wi' you!"

Their distant voices gave the whole area a sense that there was always someone around making sure you were safe.

I saw my first real live Asian child in the Gorbals — a rare sight in Glasgow at that time. She and another child were passing a ball to each other. I felt a tinge of sadness as I watched this beautiful, graceful little girl with perfect skin and glistening raven hair. She was wearing a silk outfit that made her look like something from an Arabian Nights story. How could such a delicate little flower survive in this concrete jungle? At that moment a mischievous boy ran past and quickly tugged at her pigtail. She swung around angrily, and black eyes flashing she spat out at him, "You stoap it! Ah'm tellin' ma mammy n you!" I needn't have worried, my little Asian flower could handle herself.

For women, the place of escape was the Cinema (or the Pictures as they called it). Here you could forget your problems. Once you were transported to America, where it never seemed to rain much and the houses were like palaces and no one seemed to do the washing, cooking or the ironing (except perhaps a live-in servant), then you could forget your squalid surroundings — at least for a little while.

Some people, mind you, found it difficult to pull themselves away from that world. I know of at least one mum who would go to the matinee, leaving her children playing in the street, and as it was a continuous performance she would wait on and on till the lights went up at 10 p.m. and there was no alternative but to return to her hungry children.

Throughout Glasgow, during the summer months, many evangelical organisations held short services in the open air, telling those who passed by about the love of Jesus. Our little Mission was no exception. Before the mid-week service was held the portable pedal organ would be carried to the corner of Bedford Street and Nicholson Street and forming a circle the missionaries would preach and sing to attract people to their meetings.

One occasion will forever be etched on my memory. Margaret, a 17-year-old music student stood in the centre of the circle and began to sing:

"Fairer than the morning, Brighter than the noon day,
Lovelier than the sunset upon a quiet sea.
Purer than the lily, sweeter than the bird song,
Fairest of ten thousand is Jesus Christ to me."

The sun was just setting. The weather had been kind and now the sky was celebrating the end of a beautiful day. From our vantage point on the corner, we could see the fiery, crimson sky blazing between the dark decaying buildings. As Margaret sang, my eyes followed the soft white swirls of remaining cloud and I gazed entranced at the splendour of a golden glow which beamed its reflected glory on windows, making whole buildings appear to come to life. People stopped to listen and the sweet strain of the song seemed to reach out to them. At that moment the Saviour was revealing himself to the people of the Gorbals. It was a hallowed moment I would never forget.

The next few years were to see many changes, not least of which was the disbanding of the Mission's activities in Glasgow. I was invited to a Pentecostal church and liked it so much I became a member. I later spent two years in Vineland, New Jersey, and looking back I realise that those intervening years were preparation for what was ahead.

Chapter 2
The Bible Club

When I returned from America, I couldn't wait to visit Mrs Wallace. She was now fostering three young girls whose father had died and whose mother was finding it difficult to look after them, as she also had four boys. Isabel, Mary and Maudie were three delightful wee girls who just flourished under Mrs Wallace's care.

The Mission people had turned over the flat to Glasgow Housing Department on the understanding that the Wallace family would remain, rent free. This meant that when their tenement block was due to be demolished, they would be entitled to a new house like everyone else.

As we had a catchup the girls came in with their friends. I watched them with some amusement. They were lost in their own wee world, full of chatter and giggles; in the same room but not really listening to our conversation.

Now that I was home, I shared with Mrs Wallace that I was feeling a bit lost. Two years was a long time to be away and I was feeling out of touch. She nodded over to the girls and said, "Would you not be interested in starting a Bible Club for these girls? You could hold it in the big room the missionaries used." It was like a spark that quickly burst into a flame. We immediately arranged the day and the time and the Bible Club was born.

There was a simple format. I would open with a word of prayer, followed by a time to sing some action songs while I accompanied them on the pedal organ which the missionaries had left behind. I would tell them a Bible story — asking them a few questions at the end to make sure they understood the lesson. Then the meeting would close with a final song, a short prayer and it was time for home.

* * * *

The girls brought along their friends so to begin with there were about 12 of them. I could manage that number on my own. But as winter was drawing in the local boys began to be a bit of a nuisance. They knew Mrs Wallace always made the place warm and cosy, and they began to think they would be better off at the Bible Club than on the streets in the cold and wet. Whenever I arrived at the flat, they would shout, "Kin we no' cum in?"

I would just reply sadly, "Sorry, I'm afraid you can't."

In retaliation, they began to bang on the windows, shout through the letterbox and generally be annoying. I really got to the point when I thought this isn't going to work and it wasn't fair on Mrs Wallace; after all, she had to live there. But the Lord had it all in hand.

One night, Mr Wallace returned from preaching at a Mission Hall and with him was Bill Cowan, a young man he had met there. When Mr Wallace had shared with Bill what was happening in his home, Bill said he would like to help and he was sure his fiancé (who was also called Jean) would like to help too. I was delighted, now we would be able to open the doors to the boys as well as the girls.

Jean had a lovely soft voice and a gentle way with her. She was always smiling and the children took to her right away. An abiding memory for her was how the children cared for each other. One girl in particular regularly brought her baby sister and Jean was astounded the first time she saw the wee one sitting on the girl's knee, drinking weak tea from a baby's feeding bottle, their mother had evidently run out of baby milk again.

Bill on the other hand was resourceful and enthusiastic with a loud commanding voice which was to prove very useful. Both also had what was really necessary in our work — a sense of humour.

On one occasion when most of the children had gone home, a boy ran into the room shouting, "There's a fight oot therr. They're hittin' wan anither wi' chains." We all rushed to the door and on the street right in front of us were about half a dozen teenagers lashing out at one another. Jean, Mrs Wallace and myself I were rooted to the spot, but Bill, not thinking about his own safety, dashed in between them shouting.

"That's enough! Stop it."

And amazingly they dispersed and we could hear them grumbling as they went, "It wisna oor faut."

"They started it." We realised then that this was just a case of lads protecting their territory. It was a simple matter of posturing to display their strength and no real injury was intended.

Chapter 3
Christmas

Jean and Bill worked with me for two years. But Rev. Alex Tee, an Elim Minister, was opening a new church in Paisley and they volunteered to help. The venture was so successful that they had to stop helping in the Gorbals and another young couple took their place.

Bob and I were married in August 1961 and before we knew it, Christmas was upon us. I was working afternoons only for a company who supplied first-aid goods to offices and factories. I planned a night of party games for the children at the Club and managed to get the use of Buchan Street school hall so they would have plenty of room to run around. Since they were always hungry, I thought I would also give them juice and sandwiches. I had worked out that I could make the sandwiches in the morning and wrap them in greaseproof paper so that they would be ready to take away when I got home from work.

I was so sorry that there were no cakes, but as newlyweds we were finding it difficult enough to afford gifts for both our families. I knew, however, that the kids would be glad of whatever we brought.

I woke up early and tried to light the coal fire but no matter what I did it just wouldn't ignite. I quickly had breakfast and started on the sandwiches; the fire could wait. Soon the loaves I had bought the day before were stacking up on my kitchen table and I tried not to notice as the room got colder by the minute.

A knock sounded at my door it was the Insurance man who came every month to collect our Life Insurance money. Seeing the sandwiches on the table, he asked in amusement where the party was being held. I explained and then had a wee rant about not being able to get the fire started, how it was getting really cold, and how I really needed firelighters but I was running out of time and couldn't go out to buy them. Making suitable noises he took my money and marked the amount in his book. Then he rushed out. About five minutes later, there was another knock at the door. It was the Insurance man again. He came in, went over to the fireplace and laid firelighters on the grate, covering them with coals. In no time, flames were leaping up the chimney and with a smile and a cheery "Have a good Christmas", he was gone. I was so grateful. Bob was due in at 2 o'clock so I would be able to make sure the fire was well stacked up for him coming home.

Later when I arrived at the office, I was handed a pile of, what some people would say were begging letters from every Charity you could think of. I was instructed to send a cheque to every single organisation with a letter wishing them a Happy Christmas on behalf of the Company. I can't tell you how hard that was for me.

I longed to have the nerve to charge into the boss's office and tell him about the Gorbals Club. I was choking up as I typed, imagining what his reaction would be if I brought a couple of the children to his office. He would have been astounded to know that there was such poverty right on his doorstep. While I was dutifully typing I was silently crying out to God, "Lord, if I had just one of those cheques, I could buy cakes for the children." But I knew that even if I was given a cheque there and then it would be too late to cash it, and by the time I got to the shops they would be closed.

When it was time to go home, I rushed from the office. My thoughtful husband had our evening meal ready and we gulped it down. We grabbed the sandwiches and quickly made our way to the school.

We were met at the door by one of our helpers who pointed over to a table and said, "This has been handed in by a woman called Mrs Beatson." She was a lady I knew well and was Mrs Wallace's sister-in-law. To my amazement she had made an enormous fruit dumpling for the party. Now the children would have cake. I was flabbergasted.

You see clootie dumplings are a typically Scottish delicacy, much like the English Christmas Pudding. In the traditional way they take hours to cook, (no microwaves in those days). She must have made it the day before, or even the day before that so that it would slice well and not break up.

Not for the first time God had heard my cry. In the Bible He says, "Before you call, I will answer you." I was silently calling out to the Lord in the office, but He already had the matter in hand. Yet again, someone had obeyed His prompting. I would be forever grateful.

Chapter 4
The Club Fund

The Company I was employed by was growing fast. Mr George Wallace (no relation), who was a bit of a human dynamo, started the business, selling first-aid goods to factories and offices throughout Glasgow, but he needed help with the office administration and he employed Irene Phipps, a young girl just out of commercial college.

At her interview he said, "I am looking for someone prepared to work as hard as I do. I want someone who will not be a clock-watcher but is willing to give their all to the business. If you join me, I promise you will share the rewards and eventually you may even be a Director of the Company." He was a good as his word.

By the time I went to work there as a secretary, over 30 staff occupied the premises and an army of salesmen were employed throughout the United Kingdom. Mr Wallace presided as Chairman over the Board of Directors, which included Miss Phipps (no one called her by her first name).

Here was a woman in her early 30s who had made it to the top. She was a little over five feet tall, always immaculately dressed in a well-tailored suit (with a skirt, not trousers). She wore bright colours, matching lipstick and nail polish and I don't remember her ever looking as if she needed a visit to the hairdressers. She rushed about from office to office in court shoes with just the right size of heel to be smart yet comfortable and what had kept her in the job was evidently the fact that she was first in the office and last out at night.

What we admired most about her was she never forgot she had been a humble office worker. More often than not she took our side, not in a pally way but in a fair employer way. She was always looking for opportunities to make our working lives a bit easier.

She heard the girls grumbling one morning that by the time they got to the local Stationers all their magazines were sold out. She asked them to give her a list and arranged for the magazines to be delivered every week to the office. They were laid out on the Commissionaires table and the girls paid for them when they took them home. The Stationer sent an invoice to the Company, who paid the bill.

I ordered a monthly magazine which was targeted at Primary School teachers. I found it quite useful for the Bible Club, not so much as a teaching aid but there was often an article about how children learn or one on behavioural issues. I found it quite helpful.

At the end of one month, I was laid low with a bad bout of flu. The girls had collected their magazines and mine lay on the table all alone. Miss Phipps eventually noticed and when she saw the title, she asked who it belonged to. There was a chorus of 'That's Jean's'.

She immediately responded, "Why would she want that magazine?" And the girls volunteered what they knew of the

Gorbals Club. She was amazed to discover that Isabel, one of our Office Juniors, was a helper.

When I returned the following week, I was called into her office. "Why didn't you mention your Club, Jean. We send money to dozens of charities. We could have given you a donation." I told her I had very nearly knocked on her door the previous Christmas and when she heard my story, she was shocked that they were giving so many donations to strangers and here was one of their own workers needing help. She assured me they would be helping me out in the future.

A few days later, I was called again to her office. When I had sat down, she said, "I have had a talk with the girls this morning. They have agreed that every Friday before they go home, they will put any spare coins they have in this tin." She showed me a large National Dried Baby Milk tin which had a label pasted on it that read in large letters JEAN CLARK'S CLUB FUND.

When she saw I was a little embarrassed she said, "Jean, the girls will never miss a few coppers every week, but the money will soon mount up." And then she added, "Isabel tells me you would have liked to give the children a trip to the seaside this summer."

I nodded through my tears.

"Well, you go ahead and make arrangements. And we don't want it to be a hot pie affair either. Order a proper meal. If there isn't enough money in the tin, the company will pay the difference."

I left her office in a bit of a daze. She was almost offering me a blank cheque. The following week she took me to the bank and we lodged the first lot of coppers. The account was in both our names so neither of us could withdraw what was needed without the other's signature. My feet were hardly touching the ground. In the future, every Monday our office junior Isabel would be given the task of counting out the money and taking it to the bank.

Chapter 5
Ahm No' Playin'

As World War II was over, the economy of our country was progressing very quickly. There was an explosion of traffic on the roads and as a result it was no longer safe for children to play on the streets. There had been an increase in the number of accidents and because of this the Glasgow Education Department decided to offer youth organisations the use of school playgrounds during the summer months. I requested permission to use Abbotsford Primary School and it was immediately granted.

The boys could now play football without having to stop every so often to let cars or lorries pass by and the girls could enjoy their singing games, play hopscotch or have fun with their skipping ropes without interruption.

Mary had just turned seven years old. She was always anxious to keep up with her big sister and so she refused to join the younger girls in the singing games and stubbornly insisted on playing with the older ones.

I had brought a good solid clothes rope and seeing it the girls hurriedly formed a queue so they could take it in turns to skip. But who would take the ends of the rope to get the game started? Everyone wanted to skip but no one wanted to 'caw' as we called it.

I asked one of the older girls to take an end and explained that I would 'caw' all the time and whenever anyone tripped on the rope, they would change places with the girl who was turning the rope with me. They all thought this was a good idea as this way, if anyone was 'out', it would not be for very long.

Soon everyone was caught up in the game until wee Mary mistimed her jump and was 'out'. She gamely took the rope and for a while she was happy to turn it with me but it seemed ages to her before one of the other girls was 'out'. Eventually, however, she got her chance to change places and with a big smile she joined the queue to skip.

She managed the first round without any mistakes but on the second round — catastrophe! Mary tripped on the rope again and she was 'out'. To her dismay, by this time the older girls were really into their stride and it looked as if she would be cawing all night.

Suddenly, her end of the rope was thrown to the ground. She stamped over to the school wall with her little arms folded and announced adamantly, "Ahm no' playin'!" and turned her back to us. The other girls stood wide-eyed for a minute and then we all coaxed her to try again. She cheered up when one of the other girls gallantly offered to caw for a while. But soon Mary's lack of skill let her down again. She roughly grabbed the rope and after giving it a few turns she once again slammed it to the ground and charged towards the wall, arms folded, saying loudly, "Ahm no' playin'." I don't know what made me think of it but instantly I threw down my end of the rope, stamped over to the wall and with my arms folded I said forcefully, "Neither am I."

There was a moment of silence and then as we faced the wall together, I looked down at her. She was looking at me in amazement and her little mouth was twisted as she tried not to smile.

"See how silly that looks?" I said softly. "Now stop doing this, you're spoiling the game for everyone else. You're the one who wanted to play with the big ones."

I took her little hand and led her to the rope and as we continued the game, I could see that she was feeling a bit sorry for herself.

When the next girl was 'out' I announced, "We won't ask Mary to caw again. She can't skip as well as you older girls. If she trips, she can still stay in the game." And they were quite happy with that.

* * * *

When working with children, there is always one child that you feel drawn to and to me at that time Mary was that one child. She was a little character but I had to make sure that the others didn't see her as my favourite.

One night, Mary's sister came to the Club alone. When I asked why, she replied, "Mary's in the hoaspital gettin' her tonsils oot." I found out which ward she was in and next day sent a 'Get Well' card.

A couple of weeks later, Mary came back to the Club and after about twenty minutes she saw her chance to have a wee private word with me. "You sent me a card when ah wis in hoaspital, didn't ye?" she said shyly.

"That's right," I answered. "Did you like it?"

"Aye," and then she added quietly, "Ah gave it a wee kiss every night and pit it under ma pilla."

Even yet that memory brings tears to my eyes. At that moment I realised wee Mary loved me as much as I loved her.

Chapter 6
Abbotsford Primary School

Over the years, a number of gifted people came to help. They would usually stay for at least one winter session and then as they moved on in their lives they would leave with a fond farewell. Alex Taylor was one. He was English and had been studying at a Bible College in Glasgow as he was very interested in missionary work and had plans to go to the Belgian Congo. He had already visited missionaries in France and had learned a little of the language in readiness to go to Africa, but for a number of reasons, he was working in Glasgow and would be available to help in the Gorbals for at least one session.

Unlike Bill, he was soft-spoken and I was concerned that his accent might be a problem. But the children totally accepted him. He had translated a French song into English and suggested that for a few weeks he would teach it to the children. I picked up the tune easily on the organ and he went ahead.

The title of the song was *The Saviour Loves Me* and the second verse said:

'He died to save me, new life He gave me,
He shed His blood to set me free,

41

I'll tell it o'er again, the Saviour loves me,
The Saviour loves me and I am His.

The last verse was really poignant as the words were what
was on Alex's own heart:

Now I love Jesus I long to serve Him,
I'll follow on where e'er He leads.
I'll tell it o'er again, the Saviour loves me,
The Saviour loves me and I am His.'

When at last the children had learned the whole song and
their young voices blended together, it was as if we had been
visited by the Saviour. They didn't bawl it out as they usually
did with the more boisterous songs, but they sang as if they
sensed His presence. It was a golden moment.

* * * *

It was Alex who suggested that we should apply to hold
the Club in Abbotsford School. Since we had been using it
during the summer there was a good chance the education
department would agree. It was becoming difficult for Mrs
Wallace as her girls were getting older and were beginning to
resent these children invading their space. The school was at
the other end of the street but it was centrally heated, so we
didn't need to worry about a coal fire and there was plenty of
room to have games and other activities. I applied to the
education department and was granted permission to use the
school hall and also the school piano. This was all free of
charge as we were taking children off the streets.

The school janitor was a lovely man who lived with his wife in a tiny cottage at the school gates. We had been surprised that he was so obliging but soon discovered that no one had hired the premises for some time and he was glad of the overtime.

Mrs Wallace was sad that we were going but I'm sure she realised later that it was for the best. We invited her and the girls to come and help us but they declined as they were now interested in other things. I still dropped in to see them from time to time to catch up with all their news.

Sometimes life takes an unexpected turn and we have to take stock and think what would be best for everyone. I had to do that at this point in the children's work. More children could attend the Club as the premises were much bigger and the children seemed better behaved; perhaps because most of them attended that school and they thought that since we were in the school, we must be teachers.

We could have a games time and this allowed the adults to get to know the children as they joined in the fun. Altogether it was a good move.

Chapter 7
Portobello

Now that we had money in the bank, I could go ahead with plans for the summer outing.

Although they were no longer coming to the Club, I contacted Bill and Jean to tell them about the proposed trip and as Bill had organised quite a few Sunday School trips in the past I thought it would be sensible to ask him to organise this one.

With his usual enthusiasm he launched himself into the project. Sunday School trips in Glasgow were normally to the west coast, but Bill thought the east coast would be a change so we decided on Portobello. We set the date and he booked the coach. He also arranged for the Portobello Co-operative Society to provide the catering, because as everyone said at that time 'you couldn't go wrong with the Co-op'. The only stipulation Miss Phipps had made was that the children should have a proper meal, so Bill ordered high tea with ham salad and chips, bread and butter, and a cake each.

At the Club, we told the children what we had planned and told them we would be taking a note of their attendance from now on. This was to ensure that on the day there would be no last-minute gate crashers. Needless to say, everyone's attendance record that winter was excellent.

* * * *

The big day came and forty exuberant children swarmed onto the bus. There were just six adults to look after them, Bill and Jean, Thomas Burns from my church, Isabel Geddes from the office and Bob and myself. But some older children, i.e., 11- and 12-year-olds, were also there to help look after their younger siblings.

When we arrived at Portobello with "Are we there yet?" ringing in our ears, we asked the bus driver to drop us off at the beach first as we had an hour before we were due at the Co-op. We couldn't believe how cold it was compared to Glasgow. It was the month of May but it felt more like February.

Undaunted the boys ripped off their shoes and socks and rushed to be the first to paddle in the icy waters. We had brought towels and before long we were drying the feet of shivering children who were glad to be back on dry warm ground; although they were chuffed, they would be able to tell their parents they had paddled in the North Sea.

Socks and shoes went on again and to heat everyone up we organised games. The boys played football of course and the girls brought out skipping ropes. The wee ones played singing games (In and Out those Dusty Bluebells and the Farmer Wants a Wife come to mind) so by the time we were making our way to the restaurant everyone was feeling warmer but 'starving'.

When we arrived, it was clear the Staff were shocked to see this hungry dishevelled horde converge on their premises. They were used to sedate ladies in hats, eating daintily and sipping their tea with pinkies raised. And here were our lot shouting almost in unison.

"Where's the Toilets?"

"Are thur any toilets here?"

Tables had been pushed together to make one long table in the middle of the room. Crisp white tablecloths covered the whole and white cups and saucers and knives and forks were laid on top.

Bill noticed just in time that cake stands were set out at intervals along the tables. They looked so inviting but he rushed to the manager and said, "Do you think you could have the cakes removed? If the children see them, they'll eat them first." The manager was happy to oblige.

The children calmed down as they took their places at the long table. Grace was said and then the waitresses brought in the food. I'm sure the staff had never seen food disappear so fast.

I sat next to a small boy who needed help cutting up his meal. While I was doing that a little girl on the left of me said, "Jean, what's this?" I turned around to see her holding a slice of cucumber on her fork.

"It's cucumber," I said, then realising she might not know what to do with it. I quickly explained, "You eat it."

The sweetheart looked at her fork, gave a little nod of approval and promptly popped it into her mouth. When she had swallowed it, she said, "I like that."

Many times I've thought about that moment. Cucumber is an acquired taste. But those kids were happy to eat anything.

Every plate was cleared. How different from nowadays when many children are such fussy eaters.

Once Bill saw that the children had finished their meal, he signalled to the manager and the cakes were brought in. "One cake each," Bill yelled and in seconds the cake stands were empty — no picking and choosing, any cake would do.

It had begun to rain. We had intended taking the children outside for the traditional races so Bill had another word with the manager.

"I know it's a lot to ask," he said apologetically, "but our bus won't be collecting us for another hour. Since the weather is so bad would it be possible for us to have our races in here?"

The manager smiled. "No problem," he said. "The tables fold up and the chairs can go against the wall." Every adult helped and now the fun could begin.

I have seen many an Egg and Spoon Race, Sack Race and Three-legged Race, but none of them caused as much laughter as on that day. The children tumbled and stumbled across the hall. What they lacked in skill they more than made up for in wholehearted enthusiasm. They weren't concerned about winning, they were just enjoying taking part. There was a window on the kitchen door and we could see the waitresses laughing at their antics.

While this was going on, I noticed a couple of waitresses wrapped up and slipping out the main door. Was their shift finished? Were we keeping the staff late? I hoped not.

Just before the bus was due, the remaining kitchen staff appeared with roasting tins piled up high with chips. The chef had decided to fry the potatoes he had left. All the dishes had been washed and put away but the children knew what to do. Eagerly they each grabbed a handful. This was better than sweeties.

At that moment, the waitresses we had seen leaving earlier turned up with bags of clothes. They had obviously noticed that although some of the children were warmly clad, there were others who didn't have a jacket or a coat. Some wee girls wore thin cotton dresses without even a cardigan. These lovely ladies kitted them out and the children were delighted. It was a wonderful end to a perfect day.

Chapter 8
Ballantrae

Is everything in life just by chance? I don't think so. I am a firm believer in not just co-incidences but God-incidences.

I had been running the Children's Club in the Gorbals for about six years when I read in a Glasgow newspaper that the education department was to open some schools during the summer, so that disadvantaged children could be given the opportunity of a holiday. Everything would be provided absolutely free, from beds and bedding right down to kitchen utensils; all each visiting group would need to provide was transport and food.

We had about 40 children attending every week including 15 boys between the ages of eight years and 12 years. Mary Young, a young woman in her early 20s and Jimmy Mason who was then 18-years old were my two loyal fellow-workers.

When I read the newspaper article, my brain went into overdrive. As a child I had attended a Christian children's camp every summer for six years and it was there I heard about Jesus. What an opportunity this would be. We could take the boys this year and perhaps arrange something else for the girls after the school holidays. We still had money in the Jean Clark Club Fund which would cover all expenses. I couldn't wait to tell Mary and Jimmy and was so excited when they were as enthusiastic as I was.

First, it was agreed that Jimmy would bring the boys to my house the following Saturday to sound them out. They arrived not knowing why we had invited them and not caring either. They were just enjoying the day out. But after a while I asked them if they had ever been camping. Surprisingly two of the boys said they had been at a Boys Brigade camp the previous year. They were full of accounts of paddling in a nearby burn, taking it in turns to get milk from a farm ('it wis delicious and warm!') and playing football in an enormous field. They bounced on their chairs as they talked of climbing trees, gathering wood and cooking on an open fire and as the others sat and listened eagerly, I saw longing in their eyes. I knew then I had to help the rest of them experience this other world.

The following Monday, I went personally to the education department offices and introduced myself, sending up a silent prayer that since it was now April it would not be too late to apply. When the man in charge heard why I was there he said dismissively, "This project is really only meant for school groups from disadvantaged areas and anyway we are fully booked right up to the end of June."

My heart sank but then I explained about our Club and that as far as their circumstances were concerned, 'disadvantaged' didn't even cover it. I could see his face soften. He looked at his list of bookings and then said softly, "There is a small school in Ballantrae that might suit you. A Glasgow school group will be occupying it in June. I have arranged for the equipment to be collected on the last Saturday of June but we could delay that and have the gear brought back to Glasgow the following week." Then looking steadily at me he said, "You could have the school the first week in July."

Inwardly, I was shouting 'Thank you Lord!' But in true British fashion I said calmly, "Oh, that would be good."

My heart was skipping a beat as I signed the documents. There is no way you could make arrangements as easily as that in these days, although I think the fact that we had been using Abbotsford School premises for a few years, without causing any trouble, had been in our favour.

Now I had some organising to do. I have found when something is right everything just falls into place and so it was with this project. Mary and Jimmy arranged to have the first week in July off work. Sadie, my mother-in-law, was a professional cook and when she heard about it, she said, "I'll come and do the cooking and Annie Lawson (who was her best friend) will come and help." I was delighted to have them. They themselves had six sons between them. They knew how to feed boys well. My husband unfortunately could not get time off work and our son Jeffrey was only 18 months old, but hey, the Lord was in this. We would take Jeffrey with us; everyone would help look after him. And they did.

Of all the schools in the country the Lord couldn't have chosen a better one for us — or was it just a coincidence? It was a Victorian red sandstone building with a few classrooms — just enough for us to use as dormitories. There was a kitchen, a small assembly hall with a piano, toilets and wash-hand basins with hot and cold water; this was not your usual camping in the rough. When we told them about it the boys couldn't wait to get there.

The great day soon arrived and 15 happy wee boys arranged to meet Jimmy at the bus stop at 12 o'clock. Sadie, Annie, Mary and I, complete with Jeffrey, had gone on ahead. We introduced ourselves to the janitor who seemed a bit offhand. He curtly showed us around. I discovered the piano was locked and when I asked him where I could get the key he answered abruptly, "Oh you can't use the piano. No one said anything to me about you using the piano." And with that he stamped off to his house which was just outside the school grounds. I felt sick. I had planned that at the end of each day we would have a quiet time. We would sing action choruses as we did in the Bible Club and I would tell them a Bible story. This would quiet everyone down and settle them for the night. I just felt it wouldn't be the same without the piano. But I knew enough about janitors that they were the boss and it wasn't wise to cross swords with them.

We made the beds, got used to where everything was and Sadie and Annie prepared a meal for the boys' arrival.

And right on time there they were — no suitcases or backpacks — just the clothes they were standing up in, freshly washed and pressed, and each boy had a cloth carrier bag containing toothpaste/brush, a towel, a comb, and swimming trunks. Gorbals had its own small swimming pool and as the houses didn't have baths or hot water the pool was very popular. All the boys could swim, so we had told them to be sure to bring their trunks.

Before they ate, we took them out to the playground and they were thrilled that this would be their exclusive space. And when we went around to the footpath beside the school, they were ecstatic. There in front of them was a small pebble beach and the enormous expanse of the Irish Sea. For boys who were trapped every day in the suffocating confines of grimy tenement buildings, this was heaven. It didn't matter to them that the water would be freezing cold. They were going to be the cleanest boys in Scotland.

I had a quiet word with Jimmy about the key to the piano. "Don't worry," he said. "I'll have a word with the Janny. You see to the boys."

10 minutes later, he came back with the key. "How did you manage that?" I asked.

He grinned and said, "I just told him about the work we were doing in the Gorbals with the kids. He apologised and said the last lot they had in the school were proper rogues and when he heard we were from the Gorbals he was determined to keep everything safe."

Chapter 9
Village Life

Days before we had all set off for Ballantrae, I had a good talk with the boys about how different it would be living in a village. "If you do anything wrong then everyone will hear about it," I warned. "If you break anything, or worse still steal from a shop, we will be asked to go home."

They all shook their heads fiercely, and with almost one voice said, "We wouldn't do that Jean." Nevertheless, when they asked to go to the shops, after they had scoffed their first meal, Jimmy said he would go with them.

Other than the Baker, the Grocer and the Butcher, there was only one Stationer in the village, so Jimmy led them in there. The lady behind the counter looked very agitated at first. Jimmy was to discover later that the previous 'visitors' from Glasgow had been very light-fingered and she had been told that no more Glasgow children were expected so she was shocked when our boys arrived. But to her relief she found that these boys were different.

She confided to me the next day that listening to them talking to one another about what they were going to buy brought tears to her eyes.

"Ah'm lookin' fur somethin' tae gie my M," one said.

And the rest chimed in. "Ah'm daein' the same afore ma money runs oot."

"Ah promised I'd bring ma wee sister a present 'cos she wisna cummin'."

"Ma wee brother wants a rubber and a pencil for startin' school."

The shopkeeper served them with a lump in her throat. What had really touched her was that not one of the boys was spending money on themselves. She wouldn't make a fortune from that day's sales but she would never forget the pleased look on their faces as they took away their gifts; pencils, rubbers, colour-in books for the brothers and sisters they had left behind, and of course a wee ornament for their Ma'.

On Monday, the local Church of Scotland minister paid us a visit. He told us the annual fete was being held the following Thursday on the Village Green and we were all invited. He said all the activities would be just threepence a go. I said we would be delighted This would be a new experience for the boys. I could give them money from our remaining funds and they could choose what they would spend it on.

Meanwhile, they were enjoying the fun of having their own private beach. They wrote seaweed messages on the ground and re-enacted the story of David and Goliath which was their Bible lesson the previous night. They enjoyed a plunge in the icy waters of the Irish Sea and ended their day playing football. After the evening meal, they were all content to have their 'God time' before going to bed.

Tuesday was much the same. By this time, the little money they had was gone but that was fine because the Jean Clark Club Fund was still able to provide crisps, sweets, and ices. The local Councillor came to introduce herself. She was very nice and seemed extremely interested in the boys.

By Wednesday, I was relaxed and really enjoying our stay (perhaps too relaxed). I had been given the use of the head teacher's filing cabinet to keep our money in. I used the key to open it and withdrew my handbag. And just as I closed the drawer and pushed the button to lock it my brain went into gear and I realised too late that the key was inside and so was the cash box with the remaining money for the boys.

I rushed to the Janitor's house to see if there was an extra key and he said there was but the head teacher had it and of course he was away on holiday. Fortunately, Sadie had already taken what money she needed for the week's food and all our return bus tickets were in my handbag.

The janitor tried to console me. "The boys will still have a good time. People won't expect them to pay." But I knew it wouldn't be the same. They loved the jingle of money in their pockets and the thrill of working out what to do with it.

By next day, the whole village had heard of our plight and our friendly local Councillor paid us another visit. Handing me a paper bag she said, "The people in the village were so sorry when they heard about the filing cabinet. They had a wee whip-round and have sent me to give you this money so the boys can have a good time at the fete today." I couldn't thank her enough. I know the villagers would be getting their money back but it was such a lovely thing to do. I divided the money equally among the boys and what a day they had!

The usual stalls had been set up with games to play to test their skills. There were cans stacked up to be knocked down by a soft ball and they had a go at pinning the tail on the donkey. Each of them invested threepence on a stall that invited them to 'guess the name of the doll'. It would have been a great prize to take home for a mum or sister, but sadly none of them could think of the right name.

Undaunted, they wandered around until they spied a great big pole which sat upon two sturdy trestles. Usually, the men of the village competed on this while everyone cheered them on. Two men would sit stride the pole, facing one another about a metre apart, and with a pillow they would try to knock their opponent off the pole. I have to point out however that the pole was extremely slippery, having been rubbed down with wax furniture polish until it shone.

When our boys saw two of the men having a go, they couldn't wait to try it themselves. I can't describe to you how funny it was to see the boys struggling to keep on the pole. As they launched out at each other they would both slide off but determinedly they would scramble back up and try again.

Meanwhile, the other boys would be yelling, "Gie me a shot!"

"It's ma' turn."

They were such an entertainment that when they all had a turn and had run out of money the villagers were giving them money to do it again. We were sore laughing. It was a wonderful end to the day.

* * * *

Friday was pack-up day. After breakfast, it took most of the morning to clear up. The men would be taking all the equipment back to Glasgow on Saturday so we folded the bedding and made sure everything was neat and tidy and then we made our way to the Bus Stop.

We all scrambled upstairs so we could get a good view of the countryside as we travelled home. The boys huddled together in the front seats and suddenly I felt very low. My little boy was snuggled in my arms, eyes closed, sleeping peacefully, but all at once I was overcome with negative thoughts.

The boys were chattering and laughing and I thought, *Did the week matter to them? Why did I do this? They will all forget this past week and when the summer ends, I will probably find out that they have been moved to new houses outside of the city and I will never see them again.* I knew nothing then about how the body reacts when adrenalin stops flowing. I just felt a terrible emptiness of spirit. When the bus reached the Gorbals, they all clambered past me without so much as a cheerio or thank you and I felt so sorry for myself.

Wearily, I stepped off the bus at the terminus and was met by my loving husband who did his best to cheer me up. And as the next week passed, I gradually got into my normal stride.

Then one day the postman slid an envelope through our letterbox. There was a small note inside. It was from one of the mothers.

Dear Jean,

I felt I should write to thank you for giving the boys such a wonderful holiday. They haven't stopped talking about it.

I don't remember what else she wrote – those words were enough and are etched on my memory. The boys did have a great time. They, like me, would always remember the fun we had and all the wonderful people who made it possible. I read the note again through my tears and thanked the Lord that he had prompted that kind lady to send me those wonderful words of encouragement.

The Book of Proverbs 25:11 says: "A word fitly spoken is like apples of gold in settings of silver."

I now knew the meaning of that verse.

* * * *

When the Club was started up again in September 1965, many of the children, as I had expected, had been moved to the outskirts of the city. A few of our regulars were left and a scattering of new children had joined us but the numbers were really down.

Mary and Jimmy were still working with me but we were very aware that everything was changing. More and more tenements were lying empty and those that were occupied were in a terrible condition. Altogether, there was a gloomy, unsettled atmosphere.

At that time, Bob was employed as a Van Driver with the General Post Office, and they were asking if any of their employees would be willing to transfer to their Depot in Cumbernauld New Town, housing would be provided and they would cover all removal expenses. My sister and her husband had already moved to this new town and we were impressed with how fresh and clean everything was, so after much deliberation Bob decided to apply and was accepted.

Chapter 10
Pastures New

Mary and Jimmy agreed to keep things going in the Gorbals for as long as was possible, and so, in December we moved to Cumbernauld, into an end-terrace newbuild house with garden. I was five months pregnant and was ready to enjoy this new venture.

The nearest church of our denomination was in Kirkintilloch, so our pastor introduced us to the young couple who were running the church there. John and Vera were originally from Birmingham and by this time they had been in Kirkintilloch for about eight years. They welcomed us with open arms, literally, and we discovered that they were also expecting their second child in June.

They had worked tremendously hard to build up their church. There were about 50 adult members and approximately 100 children in the Sunday School. Every Tuesday about 60 children attended Bible Club and there was a Bible Study/Prayer time on a Thursday for the adults. We were really enjoying the fellowship and by now we had bought a car so we were finding it easy to travel back and forth.

Everything was going well and then without any warning at all, on 8 April 1966 our second son was stillborn. We were devastated. It must have been really hard for Vera when her baby was yet to be born, but she came to the hospital to offer support and I was really grateful.

I have to say here that my sister, Esther, was a tower of strength at that time. She was on my doorstep every day, making sure I was alright, even though she had two small children of her own to look after.

After only a few weeks, I went back to the church, strong in body but emotionally weak; however, I was determined to help John and Vera wherever I could.

John was pleased to see us and cautiously asked me if I would feel well enough to take over the children's work till Vera's baby was born. I had already considered suggesting that to them, so it felt like confirmation. What we didn't know was that fairly soon after their baby girl was born, they would be transferred to a church in the north of England and by Christmas we would have a new pastor. I was taking over the children's work for much longer than I had anticipated.

As a child, I loved to perform on stage. For four years I had dancing lessons and later elocution lessons. The Mission I went to in my early teens were great believers in learning through doing, so in the Sunday School they had a large wooden chest containing dressing up clothes. We would be handed a Bible with the instructions, "Read this story. You will be the woman who touched Jesus' garment. Allan will be Jesus."

And then turning to a couple of the boys they would say, "You will be disciples." We were later taken into the main hall to improvise in front of the other children. It was great fun and it worked. But I never had the nerve to try it out on the children I worked with.

In Kirkintilloch, however I did decide to have a Nativity Play in spite of a great deal of negativity from the adults.

"We tried that. They're too shy."

"We kept telling them to speak louder. They wouldn't do it."

"It's a waste of time."

Nevertheless, I went ahead and it was very successful. "How did you do that?" I was asked.

Well, first of all I made sure they knew their parts. There are always children who for one reason or another find it difficult to learn their lines. I have always given them some time at the Club to privately go over their part with one of the workers. When they were rehearsing, I also told the children to SHOUT out their words to the back of the hall. This works better than asking them to speak louder.

If they had to do some moving around or acting, I would show them what to do by doing it myself. I'm sure when the child saw my poor efforts, they thought 'I can do better than that!' Which they always did. And I constantly told them how well they were doing (a little encouragement goes a long way).

* * * *

Now that I had discovered the Kirkintilloch children enjoyed performing, I decided to close the session that year with a presentation entitled, 'The Good Ship Salvation'.

I had found the script in an old book and I looked back to my own childhood to resurrect some suitable songs.

I'm afraid when I launch a project like this, I become totally absorbed in it till it's completed. Many a Sunday while the pastor was preaching, I was looking at the platform and mentally working out how I could make it look like a ship.

I knew the desk the pastor was leaning on could slide out, leaving a wooden panel on each side. I could see a lifebelt hanging on each panel (made of cardboard of course). The space between could accommodate a steering wheel (cardboard again) and I could fix a large cardboard funnel to the back wall of the platform. If I put two very large sheets of cardboard together and stood them in front of the platform it would create a triangular keel and portholes stuck on each side would give a nautical touch. I even had it colour co-ordinated, the cardboard would be covered with brightly coloured crepe paper trimmed with gold and black. There was no stopping me.

Every Tuesday I concentrated on the programme with the children, and at home I regularly scoured local shops, asking if they had any large cardboard boxes they were throwing out. I found that the cardboard crates that Corn Flake packets came in, were the best size.

I had a black skip cap at home which would be ideal for the child who was playing First Mate, perhaps they would have a blazer, and it would be great if the other children had some kind of uniform. I thought about the sailor type caps used by the Life Boys. They had just recently changed their headgear to forage caps. I wondered if they had any of the old caps left.

Next day, my longsuffering husband drove me to the Boys Brigade shop in Glasgow. The shop assistant was delighted when I asked about the caps.

"How many do you want?" he asked. When I said how many I needed and added that we would return them as soon as the show was over, he replied, "You can keep them if you like. They are no use to us now." But I politely declined as I would have nowhere to store them.

The Sunday before the programme was due to be shown, we had a last rehearsal. I asked the children if they would wear their navy-blue school trousers and skirts and a white school shirt for the show. But I added, "If you can't do that just come anyway. Don't be telling your mum you've GOT to have them."

As I would be playing the organ for the evening service, I stayed with some of the young teens after the children went home. I always brought enough sandwiches and cake for everyone and it made the young people feel special. Bob took Jeffrey home. He had arranged for David, one of the members, to take me home after the service.

During the service and as the pastor preached, I tried not to let my mind drift to next week's programme. I took my place at the organ for the final hymn and relaxed as the pastor closed in prayer.

Suddenly, an angry voice boomed from the back of the hall, "Whit right huv you tae tell ma weans they've tae wear a white shirt fur this thing next week?" It was Margaret whose three children would be taking part.

I tried to explain that I had made it clear that those who didn't have a white shirt could come anyway.

"That's no' the point," she argued. "Ma weans wulnae want tae be different fae everybody else. Their school shirts are blue. Where dae ye think ahm gonna get money fur three shirts?"

66

And I lost what else she said in a flood of despair and embarrassment.

Having said her piece Margaret stomped out and her husband followed. The congregation sat in awkward silence. David quickly gathered my bags and I followed him out to his car. I sobbed the whole road home.

Bob was livid when he heard what had happened. "Don't go back. Let them get on with it," he cried. And that would have been so easy. But I couldn't disappoint all those children. They had worked so hard.

I went back the following Sunday, taking all the scenery with me and much to my relief I noticed that Margaret's three children were in the Sunday School. After all the children had gone home the teachers and teenagers stayed behind to set everything up. When we had finished and we were enjoying a well-earned cup of tea, we couldn't stop looking at the platform. Our ship looked amazing.

When the children returned their wee faces lit up. There was a chair on board for everyone. This was going to be a very special night.

There was an excellent turnout of parents and church members and the children who took part really excelled themselves. I think the fact that they felt they were on a 'ship' helped a lot. They loved their sailor hats with HMS GOOD SHIP SALVATION printed around the brims. And in spite of the fact that there was no sound equipment in our church, the audience heard every word.

When the night was over and just as I was turning to step down from the organ, Margaret and her husband stood beside me. Before I could say anything, she blurted out, "Ah want tae apologise. Ah feel terrible. You did aw that work and aw ye asked me tae dae wis get white shirts. Ahm really sorry." Her husband quickly added, "That was amazing. You could have charged a ticket for that." I could only smile.

Amazingly, by God's good grace, we all managed to put the incident behind us and became good friends.

Chapter 11
Memory Verses

When I was a child, Scotland was known as 'The Land of the Bible'. We were proud of our Covenantor heritage and determined to stay true to the Word of God. Every child had a King James VI version of the bible, they needed it for school as well as for Church. Unfortunately, with the passage of time this version was becoming more and more difficult to understand when people no longer said thee, thy and thou. To simplify matters, the Church encouraged everyone to memorise verses. It was like taking bite sized pieces of the bible and chewing over them.

Religious education was compulsory in schools. In Primary School my class had to memorise the Ten Commandments, the 23rd Psalm, the Beatitudes, and the 13th chapter of 1st Corinthians. Children were not surprised therefore, when in Sunday School or Bible Club we gave them short, but essential, verses to learn. The only difference was that we often gave them little prizes as an incentive, such as a pencil, a rubber, a ruler, or a bookmark — all stamped with a bible verse or motto.

We made learning the bible into a game. We would chalk a verse on a blackboard, have the children chant the verse a few times and then rub out a couple of words. They would chant the verse again, mentioning the missing words, and then the teacher would rub out another word or two. This process would be repeated until there were no more words on the board.

We would then ask a few of the older children to stand up and say the verse. Sometimes they hesitated a bit over the words but that was OK. It was amusing to see the other children silently mouthing the words to encourage them. In this way all the children were going over the words again and learning them.

As time went on, we got more creative. I remember we set up a clothesline with cardboard gingerbread men pegged to it. Each 'man' had a word on his chest. Using the same system, every time the children chanted the complete verse, we withdrew one of the 'men' at random till the rope was empty. Then we pegged them all back again to repeat. There were countless variations of this, it was just limited by our imagination.

The summer was coming to an end and I knew that quite a few of our Sunday School students were soon going on to Secondary School. I knew it would be useful for them to know the Books of the Bible. I decided to go ahead with this before all the children separated into their various classes. I didn't expect the younger ones to learn them but I felt it would cause less of a disturbance if they were all together at this point.

I wrote on the board the name of the first six books. When those who could read spoke out the books a few times, I gradually deleted the names. The children then all went into their classes.

Next week I wrote more books on the blackboard, but I had deleted Genesis and Exodus, and added a new fifth and sixth book — so it read Leviticus, Numbers, Deuteronomy, Joshua, Judges, Ruth. But when it was time to speak them out, they started with Genesis and Exodus and then read right down. Gradually they were remembering them. As you can imagine this took many weeks to complete and I was a wee bit unsure that they had really learned them.

Until one Sunday as we were going home in the car, Bob and I couldn't believe our ears when our four-year-old son sat in the back seat chanting, Genesis, Exodus, Leviticus, Numbers, Deuteronomy, Joshua Judges, Ruth, and we held our breath as he carried right on through the Old Testament, into the New Testament, right down to Revelation (and even now in his fifties he can still remember them). I knew at that moment that if my wee son could remember them, then the other children would too.

In those days, to reinforce the lesson, the teacher would go over the story again, asking questions. One pastor's wife was in charge of the under-five-year-olds and she decided to tell them the story of Samson and Delilah. It came to question time and she got to the point where Samson was betrayed.

"What did Delilah do to Samson?" she asked.

And one of her tiny pupils answered, "She gied him a Kojak." (The most popular TV detective at the time.)

The way of learning the Bible that the children loved most was singing action songs. *Round the Walls of Jericho, The Wise Man Built His House upon a Rock, Mr Noah Built an Ark, Listen to My Tale of Jonah and the Whale, Twelve Men Went to Spy in Canaan*; countless songs that helped to keep the Bible stories in their minds. These methods may be considered old-fashioned in the light of today's technology but they worked, and I sometimes worry that we are treating children too much like adults and think they are more mature than they really are.

Chapter 12
Mother's Day

The Mission I attended when a child had its origins in Wisconsin, USA. Mothers' Day was celebrated there in the month of May every year, and so the missionaries thought that as it wasn't celebrated in Scotland at that time, it would be a good idea to have a Sunday School programme in which all the children would take part with poetry and songs about mothers and at the end every mother would be given a little plant to take home.

It was stressed by the Sunday School teachers that our mothers HAD to be there, so my brother, sister and myself constantly reminded our mother of the date until she got to the point of saying, "If you tell me one more time about the Sunday School programme, I won't go!" That shut us up.

Unfortunately, I became ill with flu just before the important day. I was so worried that my mum might find it an excuse not to go, but my aunt volunteered to stay with me while Jackie and Esther took our reluctant mum to Sunday School.

My mother was pleased with the welcome she was given. The teachers had visited our home a few times and they greeted her like a special friend. She saw a display of plants laid out on the platform and thought how lovely they looked. She was quite touched when she heard the children extol the praises of motherhood in verse and song, but it was the closing part of the programme that really made the biggest impact.

It had been arranged that this was the moment every mother would be presented with one of the plants on the platform. One by one the name of the mothers would be called out and the eldest child in the family would be handed a plant by the head teacher and they would then take it to their mother and say, "Happy Mothers' Day", giving them a wee kiss.

It was only then that Esther realised she would be the one to hand our mother her plant. She was thrilled.

You see Esther was the in-between child. If anything was organised for younger ones, Jackie was it. If only the oldest was invited (and this happened at two family weddings) then only Jean went. I'm sure the thinking was, "The other two won't mind." But Esther did mind. I was only a year older than she was.

But here at last was her big moment and she carried it out with a flourish. For weeks afterwards she talked about it to anyone who would listen, and even yet in her eighties she could tell you about it and still feel the excitement of that moment. A little thing that meant so much.

As for our mum, she had been given a plant that had really unusual leaves. She carried it home as if it was a new born babe and she nurtured it for many years.

* * * *

Thanks to the fact that the Greetings Cards industry was becoming increasingly successful, the idea of Mothers' Day was beginning to emerge in Scotland in the 1960s. My mind went back to that programme in the forties and I thought it would be good to do something similar. Knowing nothing whatsoever about plants I decided it would be better to give flowers and since it would be in the Spring, daffodils would be perfect. There was still £6.00 in the Jean Clark Club Fund, but if that didn't cover the cost then I would just top it up myself.

The children were becoming quite expert at learning their lines and I had unearthed some poems about mothers. As there were no costumes to worry about and they already knew most of the songs, the programme was put together quite quickly.

My father's cousin was Superintendent of the Fruit and Flower Market in Glasgow so he introduced me to a Florist who gave me a good deal and also supplied me with a generous amount of florist's paper. Looking back, I'm amazed. £6.00 would hardly pay for one bunch of flowers nowadays.

Next day was Sunday and the final rehearsal at Sunday School. The children were all told about the flowers, that they must keep it a secret and of course that their mothers HAD to be at the church with them by 6 o'clock. I knew some of them might let it slip but most of them would manage as they only had to keep it to themselves till the evening.

When the children went home, I got the boxes of flowers and sheets of paper out of our car and with the help of our wonderful teachers and teens the flowers were wrapped in bunches of five daffodils instead of six. This was to make sure we had enough for all the ladies. I had brought strong cardboard which I folded and covered with green crepe paper. Using strong double sided adhesive tape I secured it to the floor, making what looked like a large window box along the bottom of the platform. In that, we placed the bunches of daffodils, just letting the heads show. (I was told afterwards that everyone thought they were for decoration only).

All the mothers turned up and of course our church members. My five-year-old son, who was sitting with me next to the organ, was so excited about the flowers that after every item of the programme he would tug at my skirt and say, "Is it time? Is it time?"

But at long last, it was time and one by one the families were called out. Remembering my sister, I had arranged for all the children in each family to present the flowers together, suggesting that the youngest should hold them. They were happy with that.

Once all the mothers had received their flowers the pastor asked any ladies in the company, who had no children with them, to raise their hands and our teachers gave each of them a bouquet also.

Then I asked, "Is that everyone now? Is there any lady who doesn't have flowers?"

And to my dismay they all pointed at me and shouted, "You!" They all laughed but I was so annoyed with myself. I had been so caught up in the moment I had forgotten about my own little boy. He had been desperate for his name to be called and had to wait till the very end.

The pastor called him out and his little face shone as he took what was almost the last bouquet. The congregation must have sensed my regret, because everyone cheered and clapped loudly as he gave me the flowers with a kiss.

Through the years I was always careful not to show preference towards my children, but I learned from that night that I must always ensure that they were not left out either. It became a golden rule.

This turned out to be the last programme I produced in Kirkintilloch. At the end of June my daughter Beverly was born and for a number of reasons I reluctantly had to withdraw, not only from the children's work but also from the church itself. As things turned out Beverly didn't keep well for most of her first two years, so I concentrated on family and home. It seemed that the Lord was giving me a Sabbath — time to wind down and deepen my walk with Him.

Chapter 13
Cambuslang

In January 1970, we moved to Cambuslang as my husband had a new job in Blantyre and we became members of the Assembly of God Church, Bridgeton, as it was the nearest Pentecostal Church to us.

A year later, when Jeffrey was seven years old, he was enrolled in the Cambuslang Life Boys (the junior section of the Boys Brigade), so that he could have the company of boys his own age. Harry Lennie was the officer in charge and he said if I brought Jeffrey to the church hall each week, he would bring him home afterwards.

My son had only been attending for a few weeks when Harry noticed him standing at the piano quietly fingering the keys. He asked Jeffrey if he could play and his reply was, "No, but my mother can play." That night when Harry brought my son home he asked if I could possibly play for the Girls Brigade. The lady who usually played had apparently told them she could no longer attend every week, although she would be glad to play for their Display if she was needed.

This particular Girls Brigade Company had been run for almost 25 years by Harry's wife Jean and sister-in-law Cathy.

There were about 80 girls in the Company and also twelve enthusiastic young Officers who had come through the ranks.

Harry took me along the following Monday to meet with Jean and Cathy and I could see that the sisters were much loved and respected by all the girls. There was such a friendly atmosphere and I immediately thought to myself, "I really must help out here."

"You could bring your wee girl with you," Jean said. I explained that she was not yet three years old.

But undeterred, Cathy interjected, "We find the earlier they come, the longer they stay."

Because I would not be home until 10 p.m. one of the mothers whose little girl was in the Juniors, volunteered to take Beverly home to her dad, and that would allow me to stay all evening (the Explorers and Juniors went home at 7:30 p.m.).

Although I was not a great pianist, I was better than nothing and both sisters were delighted when I agreed to play the piano every Monday until the Display in May. They were also relieved when I assured them, I would be happy to hand over the responsibility to the other pianist on the big night.

I knew nothing about the Girls Brigade, but I was soon to discover that there were four sections — the Explorers, the Juniors, the Seniors and the Brigaders. The only group I would not be playing for would be the Explorers.

Although Jean Lennie also worked with the older girls when the younger ones went home, she was in charge of the Explorers, and I marvelled at the wonderful action songs she could unearth to teach the little girls their numbers, days of the week, and so on. My favourite was:

Monday is washing day, rub-a-dub-dub, clothes in a tub.

Monday is washing day. That's what we're doing today.

Tuesday is ironing day, press-a-press-press, a suit or a dress.

Tuesday is ironing day. That's what we're doing today.

Wednesday is sweeping day, broom-a-broom-broom, all over the room.

Wednesday is sweeping day. That's what we're doing today.

Thursday is dusting day, tables and chairs, up and down stairs.

Thursday is dusting day. That's what we're doing today.

Friday is baking day, beat-a-beat beat, make the cake sweet.

Friday is baking day. That's what we're doing today.

Saturday is dancing day, la, la, la, la, la, la, la, la.

Saturday is dancing day. That's what we're doing today.

Sunday, we go to church, ding-a-dong ding, hear the bells ring.

Sunday, we go to church. That's what we're doing today.

They would have a few singing games, action songs, a Bible Lesson and formation marching. Altogether it was a fun time and the little girls loved it. Bev told me in later years that she thought she had been brought along to help Jean!

The Juniors had a programme that was divided into four sections — Exercise, Bible Lesson, Marching, and whatever they would be doing for the Annual Display.

The Seniors and Brigaders had a similar programme to the Juniors but at a more senior level. The Display gave all of them a focus. Many of the older girls also worked towards the Duke of Edinburgh Award Scheme and already a few of them had achieved the Gold Award. It was a fantastic setup and I felt so privileged to be part of it.

The first year I enjoyed the luxury of fitting in with whatever Jean and Cathy wanted. They had great ideas and it was lovely being part of something so well run. The second year, as well as playing the piano, I was able to participate more in the 'ideas department'. During the third year I was accepted as an Officer and I was asked to head up the Juniors Section.

This was where I was to discover that creativity breeds creativity. We don't need to fear running out of ideas. As we use our imagination, ideas flow, and as we continue to be inventive, we see possibilities in everything around us. I now looked at the Juniors with new eyes.

I had noticed that every week they dutifully did their exercises, copying two of our young officers as I played the piano, but were showing very little enthusiasm. I suggested to the other officers that it might be fun to diversify a bit. They agreed, and so I made up two crepe paper 'shakers' for each child (eighty altogether). They were not quite up to American Cheer Leader standards, but the girls thought they were wonderful and they cheerfully swung them around as they did their exercises, keeping an eye on the young officers who were leading, while I played a medley of tunes from the film *Mary Poppins*. The girls worked hard and the result was a good item for the Display.

An idea came for the next Display, when I saw on TV little Chinese girls doing exercises using fans. I scoured all the Wallpaper shops, which were numerous at that time, and searched in their sample rolls boxes for oriental type patterns. I told Cathy about my idea and she suggested that all the young officers should gather in her house to help. I was really grateful, because I also had to make 40 paper carnations for their hair.

We all enjoyed working together although when we were knee deep in wallpaper fans and tissue paper carnations (not to mention paper cuttings), Cathy laughingly said, "Whose bright idea was this?"

On the night of the display, there was a gasp as the girls shuffled in wearing pyjamas, flowers in their hair and waving their fans. With serious little faces they did their exercises to the tune of *Happy Talk* from the musical 'South Pacific' and their friends and families were charmed.

I should mention here that when children perform, they never but never make a 'mistake'. You see, everyone is only looking at their child and thinking to themselves, oor wean's the best wean.

We always had to produce a fun item for the big night and it could be a bit of a challenge thinking of something that would include 40 girls. I thought Ten Little Sailor Boys would be good if the Life Boy hats were still available — and believe it or not, after all those years — they were!

The song has ten verses and we managed to include all the girls by including some as beehive keepers, woodsmen chopping sticks, sailors sailing out to sea, and so on. We altered some of the words to make the song less gruesome and when it came to the part where we had 'One little Sailor Boy living all alone' we put in *He Got Married* and I played *Here Comes the Bride* as our tiniest Junior appeared, wearing a beautiful little wedding dress. I had originally thought we could borrow a First Communion dress from somewhere but Alice, one of our senior officers, was a professional seamstress and she made the gown and veil exactly to size. Everyone gasped and then clapped as 'bride' and 'groom' walked arm in arm around the room as I played.

The previous week I had spoken to the mother of the little 'bride' and explained what was to happen and suggested she might like to bring a camera to take some photographs. Unfortunately, in the rush to get the rest of her family there, she forgot! (But I'm sure Cathy sorted things out.)

Cathy said that one of the keys to having a successful youth group was encouraging them to use their initiative and allow them to be creative. If they had an idea for the display she would use it, and if it worked, she would be full of praise. But she had discovered that if it wasn't working while they were rehearsing, the girl who suggested it would be the first to say so.

I had found what I thought would be a good action song for the girls to learn. "Jenny Jenkins" is a folk song with a tongue-twisting chorus. At first, I was going to leave out the chorus but when I looked back on my own childhood (a good place to start) I remembered how much we enjoyed singing silly tongue-twisters. It would also be an item that all 40 girls could take part in. We would just need one Jenny Jenkins and the rest could wear sashes showing different colours. The song went like this:

Will you wear white, oh my dear, oh my dear.

Will you wear white, Jenny Jenkins?

Oh, I won't wear white for the colour's too bright

Chorus

Gonna buy me a foldy-roldy, tildy-toldy,

Seek-a-double use-a cozza roll to find me.

Roll Jenny Jenkins roll.

Once they had learned the song over a few weeks, I asked the girls to form a big circle and gave each of them a coloured sash to wear (either white, blue, yellow, green, or red). Jenny Jenkins stood in the middle of the circle (without a sash). As the song progressed, when the girls heard their colour mentioned, they would enter the circle, walk around Jenny Jenkins and go back to their places. In between each verse the Chorus would be sung and this would give the girls time to do so.

One night the young girl who was Jenny Jenkins came to me and said she had a good idea for the last verse. I had a word with Cathy and she giggled and said, "Jean, are you trying to get us the jile (jail)." But then she said, "Go on, tell her she can do it."

84

On the display night, the Juniors formed the circle wearing their sashes and our little Jenny took her place in the middle, wrapped in a large bath towel.

The girls sang their hearts out and when it came to the last line Jenny shouted, "IT'S NOTHING I'LL WEAR, I'M GONNA GO BARE!"

The audience let out a scream as our Jenny Jenkins quickly dropped her towel, showing her wearing a little pink bathing costume.

I don't know who got the biggest shock, but I remember a red-faced Jenny hastily gathering up her towel and disappearing as fast as she could to the changing rooms while the audience laughed and applauded loudly.

I hope I am not giving the impression that everything went smoothly. There were many setbacks. At one display, I sat down at the grand piano and discovered to my dismay that about six or seven of the keys wouldn't make a sound. Consequently, no matter what I played, it sounded like a child giving the piano an occasional thump.

And there was the time Cathy thought it would be a good idea to use a cassette tape for the Country Dancing item, and the tape broke.

Oh yes, and there was the time we decided to replicate Magic Roundabout and the portable mike we used for the Narrator wouldn't stop making piercing noises.

But none of those difficulties could match the morning that Cathy's husband arrived home from nightshift to find our beloved Captain had died in her sleep, she was 46yrs old.

It would take too long to tell you how we all moved on from there. The girls had to face many changes in the next year, coping with their grief and deep sense of loss. Their little church was under the umbrella of Home Missions and their Minister had died of a heart attack a short time before Cathy. Behind the scenes the Church of Scotland, therefore, were making plans to close the church down and membership was to be combined with the local Parish Church in Flemington. This church also had a Girls Brigade company, so it seemed sensible to now join the two companies together.

Jean felt she didn't have the heart to carry on the Brigade work so she and Harry decided to become members of a church in Glasgow which they held in high regard.

I supported the young officers and girls as they made the transition to Flemington, but there were many other changes taking place. One of our lovely young officers became an Air Hostess, one became the mother of a little boy, and four got married (Sounds a bit like the Ten Little Sailor Boys — doesn't it?)

But in spite of all those changes that particular Girls Brigade Company still continues to this day.

In later years when anyone mentioned the Girls Brigade, my husband would say, with a mischievous gleam in his eye, "Did I ever tell you about the time Jean was asked to help in the Girls Brigade — just to play the piano?"

Chapter 14
Bridgeton Assembly of God

As I have already stated, when we first arrived in Cambuslang, we decided it was time to get settled in a church. We were now fairly near two Pentecostal churches — Elim in Motherwell and Bridgeton Assembly of God (Zion Hall) in Glasgow. Since we already knew many of the members in Bridgeton we decided it was only sensible to go there.

At that time, it had a high percentage of children compared to its membership. There were also around a dozen young people in their late teens/early twenties who were heavily involved in the work of the church. Bob and I were in our thirties so that put us, in their opinion, in the middle-aged bracket.

Every Sunday, I took Jeffrey and Beverly to Sunday School and I remember thinking the children were quite noisy and unruly. One girl in particular caught my eye. I judged her to be about ten years old and each week she would turn up with a large, sticky lollipop which she licked right through the Sunday School time. She seemed to believe she wasn't enjoying this delicacy unless it was smeared all over her face.

My wee girl was horrified. But I found myself praying silently, "Lord, this is the kind of child you have called me to help. Why am I sitting here doing nothing?"

But his still small voice was saying, "Not yet."

The whole area of Bridgeton was in the throes of refurbishment and restoration, just as the Gorbals had been. In fact, at one point, as we made our way along desolate streets, lined by tenement buildings that the demolishers had turned into shells, Bob remarked, "The Glasgow City planners have succeeded in doing what Hitler failed to do."

The trouble was that refurbishment in such circumstances takes time and meanwhile the children had to survive in what was fast becoming 'a ghost town'. They knew they were to be rehoused, but when and where? So, there was that familiar restlessness and uncertainty we had sensed in the Gorbals.

The young leaders were doing a good job with the children. They were using resources which were well constructed and age appropriate and according to the numbers of children attending both the Sunday School and Youth Club they certainly had a broad appeal. But young leaders usually find it hard to commit to anything for very long because their lives are in process of change. A couple of them went to university, and others got married and moved out of the city. It seemed that in a very short space of time (although it was almost two years) the church was left with a good number of children and eventually no one to carry on leadership.

I was working part-time in the afternoons at Strathclyde University but had already requested a transfer to mornings as Beverly was about to start school and working in the morning would mean that my aunt would no longer be needed to look after her. It was at this point that I was approached by the pastor and asked if I would take over the children's work. I told him that if I got the morning position in the University, I would be glad to take over. I did get it and this gave me a breathing space when I got home at 2 o'clock to see to my household chores and then I would be available to focus on the Girls Brigade on a Monday and the Bible Club in Bridgeton on a Thursday.

Here was another time in my life when all the jigsaw pieces fitted neatly together. The writer of Proverbs got it right when he stated, "In his heart a man plans his course but the Lord determines his steps." Prov. 16:9.

* * * *

Quite a few families came to Zion Hall, the oldest child would bring their younger siblings. It was a safe place and all the activities were free.

One family in particular were the Cochranes. Their ages ranged from eight to sixteen. When they entered the building, it was as if the light went on. They were all enthusiastic and helpful. I never once heard them moan or complain. They threw themselves into any and every project and big sister Ellen made sure they all behaved themselves wherever they went.

Sometimes some of the children would stay with us for the weekend. It was the time when every kid had a sleeping bag so they just bunked down on the floor. (Talk about 'take up your bed and walk!)

Zion Hall held a meeting every Saturday night so they would attend the meeting, come home with us and return to church the next day before going home. It was a great way to really get to know them.

I have to add that at no time was it suggested that the children would need a note from their parents. There was a tremendous amount of trust on both sides.

Chapter 15
Arts and Crafts

Blue Peter was a favourite television programme at that time and when I saw how enthusiastic my own two children were, when they were shown how to make something from practically nothing. I thought to myself, *We could do this in the Bible Club.*

My relatives and friends soon furnished me with margarine tubs, string, jars, cardboard rolls, egg boxes and buttons. You name it, Jean got it. I didn't refuse a thing. My aunt always said, "Keep something for seven years and it's sure to come in handy."

Every Thursday, I would arrive at the Club with bags full of 'rubbish' and after some songs and a bible story the kids would eagerly gather around to hear what the next project was going to be. Most items could be completed on the night (just as in Blue Peter) and I'm sure many a night their parents groaned when their family turned up with their latest achievement.

Margarine tubs were filled with Polyfilla and before the plaster had set artificial flowers were embedded in them. Pin pictures were being sold in the shops. Our kids had great fun hammering a design with nails into a piece of wood and then coiling thin string or cord around the nails to reveal the pattern. They learned how to make macrame plant potholders, calendars, and cone shaped Christmas trees, snowmen and angels — the list was endless.

One morning during tea break at the University I overheard some of the lecturers making scathing remarks about Blue Peter. They grinned as one said, "Who just happens to have double-sided tape in the house?"

"Or a clean margarine tub?" And then laughing they all joined in.

"Or a big supply of old buttons?"

"Or cardboard rolls or crepe paper?"

"Or a large bottle of school glue?" With every question the laughter got louder. And as they ran out of ideas and the laughter was diminishing, they were astounded to hear my little voice piping up, "I do."

Years later, I was visiting friends who also ran Bible Clubs and we had a good laugh when we looked back at our efforts to use Blue Peter ideas. I went home feeling a bit foolish. Had I been wasting the children's time? Should I have been concentrating on other things? "What did they learn, Lord?" I prayed. Then the answer came back as clear as day.

They learned to follow instructions carefully. They developed dexterity and co-ordination. They learned how to work together as a team; encouraging one another and being supportive. They developed patience, endurance and good old fashioned stickability. Was I wasting the children's time? No way!

I do remember one occasion though when our artistic efforts gave us a bit of a shock. I had been invited to a Ladies Night where there was to be a demonstration of arts and crafts.

One idea caught my imagination — Pasta Pictures. I couldn't wait to get started.

The following Thursday, I provided each child with an A4 sheet of stiff card. They could choose any style of pasta (I had an abundant supply of assorted shapes) and then use school glue to fix the pasta to the board, making any design they liked.

Their 'pictures' were then set out on a shelf to dry. The following week I sellotaped sheets of newspaper to the floor and one of the walls. I had bought three canisters of spray paint — one bronze, one silver and one gold. Each child took it in turns to place their picture against the wall and spray it with the colour of their choice. Everyone gasped as they saw the designs take on a new life. The paint dried very quickly, so they all took their pictures home that night, happy with their efforts.

There are always a few children who for one reason or another are unable to come back, this is especially true where families are being moved to new houses, we therefore had a couple of unfinished pictures and plenty of leftover pasta. I put everything in a carrier bag and placed it in a cupboard.

A few weeks later, pastor said to me, "Jean, I think we've got trouble." He opened the cupboard and to my dismay the unfinished pictures and leftover pasta had provided a feast for a family of mice!

Chapter 16
Graffiti

When we work with children, we very often forget the power of our influence.

I arrived home from a wonderful ladies conference and I was full of praise, thanking the Lord for His presence. But then I entered the common close leading to my flat and I couldn't believe what I saw. From floor to ceiling and on every wall, someone had scribbled obscene statements. I was horrified.

I dashed into my flat and grabbed a large bottle of graffiti remover and a rag, and with tears streaming down my face I scrubbed and wiped as hard as I could, but most of the graffiti stayed where it was.

My husband gently took my arm and said, "Jean, it's nearly midnight. We'll sort it tomorrow." And sobbing I let him lead me into our flat.

The next evening saw me at the Bible Club and I was still so upset that I told a few of the adults about the night before. As they were all sympathising with me, 12-year-old Calum butt in and said scornfully, "Everybody's close is like that!"

I turned on him and said emphatically, "No! everybody's close isn't like that. Where my mother lives there's no graffiti."

"Where's that?" he asked, probably wondering where this Utopia could be. And I told him.

When I returned home, I felt really bad that I had been so snappy. I felt so annoyed with myself. I prayed to the Lord for more patience and understanding.

* * * *

It must have been six or seven years later that one of the Cochrane girls decided to get some of us together for a bit of a reunion. Calum was there. He was now a young man and was evidently doing very well. I knew he was pleased with his life when he said, "Ahve jist moved tae a new flat."

When he told me where it was, I replied, "That's near where my mother lives."

He looked at me with a self-satisfied smile and a twinkle in his eye and said, "I know, and guess whit…there's nae graffiti in ma close."

Chapter 17
The Zionairs

As children approach the teen years, how do you keep them coming to church? I thought it might be a good idea to form a singing group. This would give them an opportunity to grow in their faith and would increase their self-confidence. It would also give them an understanding of what it means to serve the Lord.

The name seemed an obvious choice because we were all attending Zion Hall and on the basis that 'if you look like a choir you will sing like one' we eventually put together a uniform (floral maxiskirts and white tee shirts for the girls, white shirts and ties for the boys). After each 'performance' I would bundle the girls' costumes in a case and take them home to wash and iron for the next time.

Maxiskirts were in fashion, this was the seventies, so our girls felt great in them and it meant that no one was looking better dressed than the others. One church member got so carried away she crocheted pink berets for the girls. My first reaction was to say, "Hats are a bit old-fashioned now," but she was so happy that she was contributing I didn't have the heart to discourage her; after all, this was her church too and the more people getting behind the project the better, and since the girls were quite happy to wear them, then why not?

When I attended the Mission as a child, I was taught countless gospel songs and now in my forties I was discovering that Psalms, Hymns and even Paraphrases were coming to mind and were a great source of comfort, healing and encouragement when I had to face life's struggles. I therefore determined to teach songs to the children with their future in mind. They would memorise the words so that as the words reached into their hearts their trust in God would become stronger.

At that time Country and Western music was very popular. It was an easy form of music to learn and harmonise to, and most of the singers ended their recordings with a gospel song, so I bought a few tapes and selected songs which would tell the story of someone's faith and were also catchy and fun to sing — after all they were only children.

At first, they were performing in Zion Hall every so often, but after a while our pastor was getting phone calls from other churches asking if the children could sing there, and as they all loved to perform, he of course said he would be delighted to bring them along. They were transported in a hired minibus, so that added to the fun.

We practised every Sunday before the evening service and their repertoire began to grow. We were invited to take part in the Scottish Band of Hope anniversary programme and the audience smiled as they sang *Jesus, I Heard You had a Big Yard* and *Five Rows Back*.

Soon I was thinking up short presentations. There was an overall theme, our pastor would do the narrative which the children would interlace with songs, and pastor gave a short epilogue at the end.

On one memorable occasion they were closing by singing *I'm Gonna Sit at the Welcome Table* when the song seemed to have a life of its own. The pastor signalled to the audience to join in and as they got to their feet and added to the joyful sound it seemed as if even my little keyboard was playing by itself. We all went home that night feeling we had experienced a little touch of Heaven.

* * * *

Years later, I found out that two of the Zionairs had married two brothers and apparently, they entertained their children by singing many of the songs they had learned in Zion Hall. Their children also loved hearing stories about what they got up to (no doubt some things I wasn't aware of). I was delighted they could look back with affection on those days, and particularly pleased that the words of the gospel songs were still in their memory and being passed on to their children.

* * * *

Chapter 18
Watershed

Into most people's lives there comes a situation over which they have no control. It's a moment when they wake up and say, "I wish this was just a nightmare. I wish I hadn't made that choice." But we have to live through it and it's then our trust or lack of trust in God reveals itself.

Bob and I had been attending Bridgeton AOG for six years. I had just moved into another department in the University and was really enjoying the challenge. The Girls Brigade work was ticking along nicely and the children's work at church was doing well.

Totally unexpectedly we were offered a job in a town outside of Glasgow; a joint post in a children's home. My first reaction was to feel a bit tearful. I was just settling down after so many changes in my life and I wasn't sure I was ready for more. But Bob was delighted as this was a promoted post and all our friends and relatives had something positive to say.

Knowing nothing about my situation, one of the cleaners at the University shared with me her anxiety, because her daughter had just gone away as a missionary to South America taking her six month's old baby with her. This girl was willing to live in jungle conditions and here I was afraid to go to the next town. It seemed ridiculous. "And besides," I reasoned, "this would be the first time I had been paid for looking after other people's children!" (Other than when I had done some babysitting.)

To cut a long story short, we left our jobs, our home and our church. (Looking back now I can't believe we could walk away from the great life we had). Our children had to attend new schools (Beverly to Primary and Jeff to Secondary). If either of our children had been upset at our move, I am sure we would have given it more consideration but they were both excited about the prospect and so we went ahead with it.

Unbelievably we were in the post for just seven months and we were left licking our wounds. We were in shock. We had loved working with the children and we couldn't understand what went wrong. We were told that we just weren't suitable. Forty years had to pass before the Lord allowed us to know the whole story. It seems the children were being molested by a member of staff. That person was evidently afraid we were getting so close to the children they might tell us what was going on. They needed to get rid of us.

Bob and I were now classed as homeless so we were allocated a local authority house in Bonhill and we set about looking for jobs in an area where factories, offices and shops were fast closing down due to a countrywide recession. It couldn't have happened to us at a worse time. Unemployment was something neither of us had been faced with before and we were astounded when we saw a queue of men standing outside the Unemployment Office waiting to sign in. We joined the queue and when it was our turn, we couldn't believe how nasty the counter staff were. They made us feel like malingerers and to make matters worse there was no privacy — everyone heard your business.

We went home feeling like paupers and wondering where the Lord was in all of this. I felt numb. I needed to understand what was happening but I couldn't read my Bible, it was just a whole lot of words that were meaningless. We still hadn't unpacked everything so I set about opening a cardboard box and began to put the contents into our bookcase. It was then I pulled out a small leather-bound copy of the Daily Light. It had been a gift from a close friend on our wedding day.

For those who have never heard of the Daily Light let me explain; this is a book of Bible Verses. On the left page are verses meant to be read in the morning and on the right page there are verses to be read at night.

Every page has a theme with appropriate verses. For example, if the main verse for the morning is 'The Lord is my Shepherd', then the other verses on that page would be verses to do with that theme. If the main verse in the evening was 'I will never leave you nor forsake you', then the other verses on that page would be in a similar vein.

In my desperation, I made myself systematically read that little book. The pages were dated so I could discipline myself to simply read the words for that particular date. I needed answers. Why did this happen? Where would we be going now? What caused this to happen? Who could we go to for help? So many questions and most importantly, how do we pick up our lives from here?

Every morning when I woke up, I read the verses for the morning and later I made myself read the evening verses before I went to sleep. Most of the time I wasn't really taking it all in but then gradually something began to happen. One day I was thinking about our situation and I called out in despair, "Lord, why did this happen? I have always worked for you. I have helped so many people. I sacrificed so much." I felt anger erupting inside of me. Bob and I had been trying so hard to be good Christians and here we were in this predicament. It just wasn't fair.

That night I was reading my Daily Light when some of the words seemed to leap out of the page. They were King David's reply when Araunah the Jebusite offered his land for free. "I will not offer a SACRIFICE to the Lord that has cost me nothing," he said. I felt really ashamed. I had been looking after His children and now I was saying, "You owe me!"

My emotions were fluctuating, not just from day to day but from hour to hour. One minute I would feel calm and stable and the next I would be a tearful wreck. At the beginning I was saying to myself, "So what is the advantage of being a Christian if we don't have God's protection in such circumstances?" But then I seemed to hear His words, "If I could promise everyone who gave their life to me protection from all ills, there would be queues a mile long. I can't put everyone who loves me in a glass case where they are shielded from all evil. I'm looking for unconditional love."

I was reminded of Psalm 34:19, where the Living Bible states, "The good man does not escape all troubles — he has them too. But the Lord helps him in each and every one."

On another occasion, I tried to think of justifiable reasons for our situation; did we somehow bring this on ourselves? Where did we go wrong? The Daily Light that day included Mathew 27:28 "...the Jewish leaders had arrested Jesus out of ENVY because of His popularity with the people." That was a light bulb moment. I could see that may have been true in our case.

Another day I was in tears because I felt a total reject and then I read Is.53:3 "He was despised and REJECTED of men, a Man of Sorrows and acquainted with grief."

A big problem for me was what I saw as my ruined reputation. A few invitations were received from friends which I turned down because I couldn't face anyone. Our situation had been made worse because there was no specific reason for our dismissal. I could just hear everyone saying, "There must be more to it than that."

Then I read, "Christ Jesus made Himself of NO REPUTATION..." (Phil.2:7.)

We had been advised by Bob's previous employer to take the company we had worked for to Tribunal, as it was a clear case of unfair dismissal. At our lawyer's suggestion I approached two pastors I had worked with and requested letters of reference. I was really disheartened when the two letters arrived. One suggested there might be two sides to the story and the other letter said I had once worked for him, when it was the really other way around. The letters were poorly typed and I was so embarrassed. That night I read, "I looked but no one came to help them I was amazed and appalled. So, I meted out judgment." (Isa. 63:5)

We did win our case but I was still in real turmoil. It hadn't solved anything. In fact, I think it had just made everything more deep-seated. I was now being approached by people who were quick to tell me what was being gossiped about us. My little book declared, "Blessed are you when men...say all manner of evil against you falsely."

I then was faced with someone's dismissive treatment because they saw me as a bit of a failure and I read, 'A servant is not greater than his Lord', and 'Foxes have holes and birds of the air have nests but the Son of Man has nowhere to lay His head'.

"Well," I thought, "at least I have a roof over my head. Thankyou Lord."

We were now living quite a distance from Zion Hall but we wearily returned like two wounded animals and everyone gave us a tremendous welcome and assured us of their prayers and support. They graciously asked me to carry on where I had left off, so I started up the Zionairs again and travelled by train during the week to take the Bible Club.

They say when someone loses a loved one, very often those who mourn go back to where they came from. It brings comfort to visit familiar places where they once felt happy and secure. There is no doubt that is how we felt when we returned to Zion Hall.

At the end of the year, when we were praising God for a comfortable home, good jobs and the four of us had made new friends, I asked the Lord what he had really been saying to me through the Daily Light. His reply came into my heart and mind right away, "There is not a single thing you have been through that My Son has not been through also." A golden moment indeed! I had walked where Jesus walked.

The most valuable thing that came out of this experience was that I had the ability to differentiate between God's thoughts and my own. The Bible states: My thoughts are not your thoughts.

And what I didn't know then, but realised later, was that everything the Lord taught me about Himself and His Son during that year, would be used in a remarkable way a few years down the line.

Chapter 19
New Premises

We had been travelling backward and forward to Glasgow over the next two years when again our circumstances changed. The firm I worked for was purchased by another company and my boss, who was Regional Manager, was made redundant as the new company had their own management team. And since I was his Secretary, I was also paid off. My son had been working in the centre of the city but he was transferred to Queenslie Industrial Estate which meant he would need to travel by both train and bus to get there.

One of the church members became very upset about our situation. "You need a house nearer Bridgeton," she declared. "I'm going to find one for you." Bob and I just smiled. For years, Glasgow Housing was struggling with a huge waiting list, but if this lady thought there was a way, she could go ahead with our blessing. And she did!

We moved to Barlanark in December 1979. The area was very run down, hence the reason a flat was available, but the accommodation was just what we needed. It had great transport links to Glasgow, where I was now employed, Jeff's place of work was only a walk away and Bob got a job in a

Care Home in Easterhouse, a short bus ride. Added to this the local Primary School for Bev was just across the road from where we lived.

Once again, I had discovered that when you are doing what the Lord wants you to do, like the Psalmist you can say, "The boundary lines have fallen for me in pleasant places." (Ps.16:6)

* * * *

Chapter 20
Moving On

It was around about 1980 that the owners of the building paid Zion Hall a visit. They said the local authority had made them an offer they could not refuse and the building was being demolished. They suggested that the congregation have a look around the area to find alternative accommodation and they gave them a cheque for £10,000 to help with the removal.

Meanwhile, Luis Palau was coming to Glasgow and our pastor was asked to attend a pre-crusade meeting. He got to talking with a Congregational Church Minister. This gentleman was looking for someone to buy a disused red-sandstone Congregational Church building in Dalmarnock Road. The price? You guessed it, £10,000.

Yes, we moved there and as is always the case with change, some were happy about it and others not. The premises were huge compared to what we had previously. There was a set of halls attached to the sanctuary which included a kitchen, a dining room and a large assembly hall, which the boys immediately saw would be useful to play softball in.

I always kept my eyes open for opportunities to improve what we were doing with the young people and noticed in the local paper that Glasgow City Council were offering grants to youth groups towards sports equipment. I applied because I noticed they were offering grants specifically to organisations that were working with young people who the authorities considered to be living in disadvantaged areas.

A few weeks later I received a letter stating that our application was unsuccessful because they did not fund religious organisations.

I had been warned that this would probably happen but I considered it completely unfair and so I sent another letter saying, "We teach the young people, among other things, that stealing is wrong, that they should obey their parents and respect them, and that they should always tell the truth." Then I asked, "Could you tell me what we are doing wrong?"

By return, I received a cheque for £250.00 which was used to buy Netball and Volleyball equipment. Now the young people could really make use of the large hall. This also ensured that they were early for church on Sunday and Bible Club on Thursday. A wee practice beforehand and they were happy to settle down and listen when the service started.

Chapter 21
Called Out

One lovely summer's evening, I was walking towards the church on my way to the Adult Bible Study, and I was suddenly overwhelmed with love for my Heavenly Father. I thanked Him as I walked along for all He had done for me and my family. We were now living once again in Glasgow and much nearer the church. I was excited about the future and full of gratitude for the past. But then I heard His still small voice saying, "Perhaps I want you out of Bridgeton?" The words were so definite, so unmistakable I literarily stopped in my tracks.

My quick response was, "Oh Lord my heart and soul are with these people. How could I walk out of there again?" But just as quickly I added reluctantly, "You would need to work it out Lord."

* * * *

For a while, everything was flowing along as usual and then gradually the young people found somewhere else to go. Was it just that they had money in their pockets as they were now working, or was it that there were other horizons to explore now that they were growing up? Whatever the reasons they attended less and less until one Sunday evening I swallowed my tears as I realised that there were only a few still interested. There were still quite a few younger ones but the older ones had gone.

Ellen and Callum were still helping us every week but I could see the dynamics were changing and I was finding it hard to hang on to my own enthusiasm, especially when I was feeling I should be leaving too.

When I returned to Glasgow, I had found employment but I was very unhappy there. The demands were enormous and I was finding it very challenging. My father was diagnosed with cancer and my sister and myself spent quite a lot of time supporting our mother in between running our own homes. Altogether, the stress levels were very high.

An elderly lady in our church said to me one night, "I don't know what this church would do without your family." And she went on to say how everyone depended on us. She had no idea what I was thinking.

When I got home that night I prayed, "Lord how can I let Mrs Gee down? I feel so awful about this." Amazingly, a couple of weeks later pastor found a pile of letters behind the door — one for each individual member. She was just letting us know that she would not be back because she was going to live with her sister in Largs.

It seemed that every time I placed a barrier before the Lord, he swiped it away with one felled swoop.

I had, of course, shared all this with my dear husband and he said if I believed the Lord wanted us to move then he would support me, but I was worried about my children, who were now 15 and 20 years old. If they left with us, they could very well be losing touch with friends. Then surprisingly Beverly said she was unhappy because the two girls she was closest to at church were now at the same secondary school, and since Bev went to a different school she was feeling like an outsider. I was appalled when she said, "I feel so lonely, Mum."

I had a long talk with the pastor and tried to explain how I felt and he was very noncommittal. Perhaps he was saying to himself, "Well she left six years ago and came back a few months later." But we both agreed that I should leave in April. We would be attending the Annual Conference at Minehead. Bob and I would go there but not return to the church afterwards.

Two weeks before the conference, I laid my last obstacle before the Lord. They wouldn't have a pianist/organist. I felt so bad about this as music is very much a part of worship in Pentecostal churches.

I had spent the weekend with my parents and was standing at Glasgow Cross waiting for the bus to Dalmarnock when I suddenly realised I knew the woman who was also standing at the bus stop. Margaret had been organist at Zion Hall many years before I went there. I discovered she now lived in Dalmarnock and when I shared with her that I felt led to work in my own area I added hopefully, "Would you by any wonderful chance be willing to play for the people in Dalmarnock?"

I couldn't believe it when she immediately said, "Yes!" She was a much better musician than I was and she already knew many of the church members. She said she would come to the church the following week.

She kept her word and everyone was delighted. The last piece of the jigsaw was in place. I could now relax.

Chapter 22
Easterhouse

I didn't know anything about the churches in the Easterhouse area but a friend said I should visit Easterhouse Baptist as the pastor was a good man, so I thought I would start there, little realising it would be my spiritual home for over thirty years.

When I got home from the AOG conference, I paid the church in Easterhouse a visit and the pastor was away on holiday. I was made very welcome, however, and I found myself telling one of the members a little bit of my background. I later thought to myself that she must have told everyone that a strange woman had arrived saying she had a directive from God. I soon was to learn that the Church was praying for experienced workers, so my arrival with 30 years' experience behind me was not quite the surprise I assumed it to be.

When I eventually met the pastor, he told me that two young girls had come to the church about a year before this and they had a burden to start a children's Bible Club, but it was taking a long time to put together, mainly because they were unsure of how to get started. "Maybe you could help them, Jean," he said.

The girls, Angela and Susan, invited me to their next meeting and I was introduced to their proposed team. Helena was the mother of three children who ran a Bible Class for a few years when she was in her teens. She was the only one with experience. Christine was a new Christian (converted at the Luis Palau crusade), Susan was a Nurse and Angela had just completed a course at Bible College.

Angela produced a set of lovely cards, beautifully illustrated, and said we would be putting them through the letter boxes to invite the local children to join us. She then asked each person if they had any ideas of what kind of programme we should have. Each one in turn said they couldn't think of anything.

But then it was my turn. It was like oil gushing from the ground. I told them the best way to find out which children would be interested in attending every week, was to hold a Holiday Club two weeks before the children went back to school at the end of the summer holidays.

I had given the programme much prayerful consideration. Because I knew the schools were not teaching the bible and Sunday School attendance was low, the lessons would have to be very basic and easy to understand.

I suggested that the story of Noah would be a good starting point. We could divide the story into five sections and just tell part of the story each day. We could teach them the Noah song and other songs too. We could give them a craft project every day: animal stick puppets and finger puppets would be good. And pictures of Noah and the Ark could be photocopied and they could colour them in. We could introduce them to games that were all about animals. (I think the girls wondered what had hit them!) But to my relief they were very excited that now they had a way forward.

* * * *

By the end of July, all our preparations were made and we were ready. Unfortunately for various personal reasons, Susan had to leave the project, and just before the Holiday Club was due to begin, Angela was offered employment so far away she would be unable to continue. But the rest of us carried on. The street next to the church was lined with four-storey buildings that housed hundreds of children. It was now time to throw out the net and bring them in.

For the sake of the readers who have never tried a Holiday Club I will tell you how we began.

We were joined by a few church members who very kindly offered to help us deliver the post cards.

There were eight of us so that was two couples on each side of the street. I asked them to stay in pairs, go into every alternate close and to knock on the door of the first flat. They could then say who they were, where they came from and that the Holiday Club would be starting the next week. It had been a long time since the church had any personal connection with the community. If we just put the post cards in the letter boxes, they would go straight into their bins. But here we were, handing them in personally and introducing ourselves, which helped build trust.

I then suggested that they ask the first tenant on the ground floor if there were any children upstairs of Primary School age. This would save them having to knock every door in the building. Our strategy worked and saved a lot of time.

Chapter 23
Holiday Club

The EBC congregation seemed less than enthusiastic when the pastor announced the day before we commenced that we would be glad of any help, so I was amazed when the next day twelve members turned up and I had to quickly slot them into the programme.

Two of the adults were placed at the door to take the names and addresses of the children and others made them welcome and showed them where they should sit. We scattered some of the adults among the children to ensure there was no rowdiness.

About 30 children arrived. It wasn't as many as I would have liked, I knew there were a lot more children out there but I thanked the Lord and altogether things went well.

On my knees the next morning, I prayed that more children would come — about 40 appeared. On Wednesday over 50 children arrived and on Thursday 90 came! (Now I was having difficulty finding room for them all). I'm ashamed to say Friday morning found me praying to ask the Lord not to send any more! To my relief the numbers went down a little that day.

Before the children went home on the Friday, we announced that we would be holding a Bible Club in the church every Thursday, starting the week after they went back to school. We explained that since we had everyone's name and address, they would all receive a letter to remind them.

Three young teens had attended the whole week. Sharon, Helen and Linda were friends and they had been very helpful. I asked them if they would be willing to come every Thursday night to help us out and they happily agreed.

Children love to see teenagers on the team. They see them joining wholeheartedly in the activities and it gives them the incentive to do likewise. It is also good for the young teenager, it gives them a sense of responsibility, they grow in confidence and self-assurance, and it helps them cross the bridge from childhood to adulthood.

Everything was set for us to have an exciting time as we introduced the children to Jesus our Lord. We were all eagerly looking ahead.

Chapter 24
The First Two Years

Once the Bible Club was up and running, I had expected some of the children would start coming to our Sunday School. Only a very few took up our invitation. One of those was Jenny. I will never forget the first day she came. She was in my class and she was like a little sponge, soaking up everything that was said.

I was telling them about the boy Samuel and had reached the part of the story where Samuel heard the voice of God. I explained that we can also hear God speaking to us and asked, "How do you think we hear God's voice?"

And as Jenny pointed to her head she quickly replied, "In our minds."

I had expected someone to answer, 'When we read the Bible', or 'When we hear the Sunday School lesson'. I was completely bowled over. This wee six-year-old had never been to church before and here she was making this profound statement.

As she was going out the door to go home, she said to me, "Is that why we come to Sunday School, to hear about God?" I nodded and her eyes widened as she said, "I like that."

* * * *

I saw an advertisement in a church magazine for a Flannelgraph, which claimed to have figures covering the whole of the Bible. The cost was £230. It might as well have been a thousand pounds. I mentioned it to one of the Ministers who visited the office where I now worked and he said the Sunday School Union would perhaps give me a grant to help pay for it. He gave me the address and I immediately sent a letter. I received a reply stating that they only gave grants for teaching materials. I don't know what they thought a Flannelgraph was, however I discovered the Minister I had confided in was on their committee and as a result I was sent a cheque for the sum of £100.

A couple of weeks later, there was a knock at my door and one of the EBC members handed in an envelope containing £100 from the Church. Shortly after this, I was asked to speak at a Mission and on leaving I was handed an envelope with £15 inside. In the end, I only had to pay £15 — that I could manage. Praise the Lord!

Chapter 25
Revival

Meanwhile, there was a tremendous move of the Holy Spirit in our church. Every Sunday the worship songs swept everyone along a heavenly pathway. The presence of the Mighty God was almost palpable. Visitors, and there were many, would remark on how a loving spirit seemed to permeate the whole sanctuary. Many kept coming back and they brought their children with them.

The fruit of the Spirit was very much in evidence. Love, joy, peace, patience, kindness, goodness, faithfulness, gentleness and self-control, poured out of hearts that had a newfound joy.

Our Sunday School had already been subject to a transformation. We had seven teachers for every class, which meant that our teachers only missed the adult service once every seven weeks. It also meant they got to know the children in their particular class and could interact well with them outside of church.

We were using Scripture Press materials that fitted perfectly into our timetable. There were question and answer worksheets for all the children reviewing the Bible lesson and sheets with puzzles (dot-to-dot, wordsearches, etc.). There were Bible pictures to colour in, games to play and juice and biscuits to enjoy. It was a great programme and altogether a joyful time. Quite a few of the children brought their school friends for a visit (I think they were showing off a bit).

Soon, the service in the Sanctuary was 'standing room only' and many of the children were sitting on their parent's knees. As a result, our pastor and church leadership decided it would be best if the children went straight into Sunday School as soon as they arrived. Their parents could hand them over and collect them when the church service ended two hours later. This would free up seats in the Sanctuary for the adults.

I realised then why the Lord had led me to EBC. He chose a Pentecostal children's worker to take care of the Sunday School, because she could cope with the upheaval of Revival, and could be occupied with the children for two hours every Sunday without feeling spiritually left out.

Revival in the church is really for Christians. The Lord uses it to stir His church into action. EBC's Revival had an enduring effect on all of us.

Chapter 26
Glasgow A' Lit Up

I was now working as Secretary to the Youth Adviser in the Youth Office of the Church of Scotland. It was my dream job. I worked Monday, Wednesday and Friday (which made every day seem like a Friday, since I had next day off).

We loaned out Board Games, Parachutes, Books, Camera/Video equipment and countless other items — it was a veritable Aladdin's cave for youth workers. Many a discouraged youth leader or Minister would come to the office, feeling very downhearted, and after a couple of hours they would leave armed with fresh ideas and filled with renewed enthusiasm for the work.

One day, I arrived at the office and was told that Colin our young volunteer and myself were to be shown how to make lanterns. There was to be an event entitled, 'Glasgow a' Lit Up' and every school and youth organisation had been invited to take part. Thousands were expected to be there. Everyone would gather in Washington Street and march from there to Glasgow Green wielding a home-made lantern.

Colin and I were dropped off at one of the disused sheds on Clydeside and introduced to a young man who set us to work right away. We had a great time wiring our lanterns into the basic shape; inside were crosswires to hold a tee-light in place and then we helped each other paste glue-covered sheets of tissue over the frames. Canes were attached and, on the day, everyone would hold them high as they marched along.

When I eventually went home with my sample lantern, I couldn't wait to show it to Christine and Helena. They were as excited about the project as I was, so I arranged for my dear husband Bob to collect the free materials from the organisers and we got started right away.

By about two weeks before the event, all our children had made their lanterns and each one had a different silhouette of an animal pasted on. The weekend before the big day my daughter made the framework of a Noah's Ark and as she was only home from Art School for that time Helena and I covered the Ark with the necessary tissue. We attached two long canes to the bottom of the Ark and arranged for four strong young men to carry it in the procession shoulder high.

Saturday came and the rain was torrential. We had visions of the lanterns melting. But by 5 o'clock, miraculously it had ceased and we set off in cars to the appointed place. The Ark was transported in a minibus.

Our children were amazed when they saw the hundreds of people forming up, ready to take part. And they were really excited when a brass band was placed right in front of us.

A whistle blew and the march was on. Soon our kids were striding it out, marching in time to the band.

I smiled across at ten-year-old Andrew. His little chest was sticking out as he marched behind the band. As I caught his eye, he shouted above the noise, "Jean, I feel like a STAR!"

When we arrived in George Square there was a huge choir singing their hearts out and hundreds lining the pavements. It was a tremendous sight.

When we arrived at Glasgow Green our lanterns were laid around a bonfire (We had warned the children beforehand that this would happen, we didn't want any tears). But we needn't have worried there was so much to grab their attention. Huge lanterns had been installed in the Green and once everyone in the procession had arrived, there was a magnificent fireworks display while the bonfire made short work of our handiwork.

It had been a lot of work and it took a bit of organising but it was worth all the effort.

Chapter 27
Douglas West

Glasgow's children are confined to their homes or public buildings during most of the winter. The short, dark, wintry days discourage them from taking part in outdoor pursuits. Because of this, as soon as the clocks spring forward in March, there is a steady decrease in the number of children who attend indoor activities as they are hungry for the fresh air and sunshine that the longer days bring. For that reason, we usually closed the Bible Club at the end of April.

In the village of Douglas West, there was a disused school building which our church hired for weekend retreats, from time to time. We applied to have a day out for our children and were accepted. We thought it would make a fitting end to our winter session that year.

Raymond and Michelle, a young couple in our church, volunteered to do the catering and some young people from our church's youth club came to help Linda, Sharon and Helen with the games.

We didn't have funds for a bus, but kind members from the church who had cars, agreed to transport the children from the church at 11 o'clock and return for them at the school at 5 o'clock to take them home.

Everything went according to plan. They all had crisps and juice on arrival and then had great fun playing games in the playground.

At lunch time, they were called indoors by Raymond and Michelle as they had Burgers and Chips ready and as much bread and butter as the children could eat. After which they went outside again for their very own Olympic Games.

There were about 40 children and they were divided into Teams with two teenagers in charge. They all had to think of a name for their Team and also a National Anthem (something silly like a Nursery Rhyme or a Pop Song).

The events consisted of the Javelin (with straws), discus (paper plates), longest feet, shortest feet, tallest, smallest and the old races (three-legged, high jump, hop step and jump). We ended with the loudest voice shouting "Ahm ma mammy's big tumshie" (always good for a laugh).

First of all, the team leaders would take note of which event each child would want to enter (maximum of two in each event). And two adults would be responsible to see there was fair play.

I had already sprayed cardboard discs with gold, silver and bronze paint. I punched a hole through each one and threaded string through them.

After each event the first, second and third winners would stand on the podium to receive their medals and everyone would sing the gold winner's national anthem. In this way everyone felt like a winner because as they all joined in the song, they were celebrating the gold winner's achievement and feeling good about it and not resentful.

This game is great fun and gets the children interacting with each other. Unlike the real Olympics there is no real competitiveness. It's all about having fun and building relationships.

When the Olympic Games were over, Raymond and Michelle called them in for juice and homemade cakes donated by the ladies of the church.

The cars came to take them home, which was another treat as very few families in Easterhouse had cars at that time.

Altogether, it was a memorable day.

Chapter 28
Performing Again

I was visiting another church and one of the members offered to drive me home. I sat in front and her three children sat in the back seats. She put a tape into her cassette player and suddenly the children burst into song. The music was catchy, there was some dialogue and the words of the songs were mostly from the scriptures.

I hadn't heard any of the Psalty tapes before and when I saw how much my friend's children were enjoying this one, I couldn't wait to buy a set, complete with instructions for performing.

A few years later a friend of my daughter, Craig, suggested we make up a show of our own and so 'The Kingdom Kumstie Kildermorie' was born. Craig was a very talented musician and he wrote the opening song, *We're Just Full of Life*. Christine and I put our heads together and came up with the storyline about someone coming to Easterhouse to tell the children about God, which was really the story of how the Bible Club began.

Unbelievably, I wrote most of the songs — they would come to me in the middle of the night. I would wake up, creep into my living room, very quietly record the song (in case I forgot it the next day) and then go back to bed and sleep till morning. The Holy Spirit was certainly involved in this one.

It was a great success. One of the parents wrote an article in the Church Newsletter which ended with, 'This show deserves to be on the road'. We were very grateful for his kind remarks.

* * * *

Two years later, Glasgow was given the proud title, City of Culture. To celebrate this, the *Evening Times* was offering grants to groups who would put on a show. They were giving £180 to each group as well as posters, leaflets, badges, flags, hats and a large banner.

I already had an idea for a show and so it was very easy for us to apply. Our title was, 'Klowning in Kildermorie' and every act depicted one of the Fruits of the Spirit. We used the money to buy material for clown outfits and we even had a pantomime horse.

Billy Graham had quite recently come to Celtic Park and Christine and I were very touched when Ian White sang a song he had written especially for the Crusade, entitled, 'The Cross is Still There'. We had tears in our eyes when we noticed two Nuns signing to the song and realised there were two rows of deaf people just in front of us who were watching their every move. There and then we decided to include the song in our show. If the children couldn't do the signing, they could always sing it.

This was another occasion when the Lord intervened. I mentioned the song to someone who was visiting the office and miraculously his wife knew sign language. "I'm sure she would be delighted to teach your children the song," he said. And she did. She came for a few weeks until they had learned the signs off by heart.

Each child had been given a part to play in the overall programme, which meant we couldn't devote as much time practising the signing as we would have liked, so I recorded the song on tapes and a couple of weeks before the big night I gave a tape to each family; that way they could practise signing at home. One wee family rushed home with their tape and ordered their mum to sit down. They then switched on their record player and standing in front of her in a row they earnestly signed to the song. She told me later her eyes filled with tears, she was so proud of them.

Chapter 29
Retirement

I was sitting watching the children playing a game. Christine was calling out the commands and Helen and Sharon were running about with the children. Suddenly I felt very tired. I had been working with children for nearly 40 years off and on and that night I was feeling my age.

I was aware that my energy levels had been slowly dropping and began to realise that I should prepare myself for another season. Perhaps working with adults. Quite a few of the new members in our church had never been to Sunday School and so the fundamentals of the Christian faith were completely new to them.

As I sat there, I dismissed those thoughts and just carried on with the evening's programme. But a few weeks, later one of the church leaders said, "I was praying for you, Jean, and I felt the Lord was saying He wants you to minister to the Baby Christians," and he added "I don't mean children." I thanked him and told him I thought it was confirming what I had been thinking. I knew then I would have to start putting things in place.

Christine agreed to carry on the children's work and I withdrew first of all from the Bible Club and then from the

Sunday School. Reluctantly I retired from the office (I didn't want to end up working in the YOUTH office with a walking stick or a Zimmer. I think it would be bad for the image).

There followed a period of prayer and reflection. I then found I didn't need to initiate anything. I was simply asked to organise things and as in faith I stepped forward, everything fitted into place.

I found that working with adults needed less physical energy but required more brain power and wisdom and this is where, after all those years, my little Daily Light came into its own. I was standing on the Word of God. Because of my little book I was sure of my faith. I didn't know all the answers but I knew how to pass on what I believed. And I did it with confidence because I had been through a few trials along the way and found that God is Faithful.